PLATE 1

WEAVING
IS FUN

BY

A. V. WHITE

Lecturer in Needlework and Handicrafts at
St. Katharine's College, Liverpool

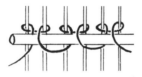

DOVER PUBLICATIONS, INC.
NEW YORK

ACKNOWLEDGEMENT

The author wishes to thank the students of St. Katharine's College for the loan of various pieces of weaving shown in the Plates of this book.

Published in Canada by General Publishing Company, Ltd., 30 Lesmill Road, Don Mills, Toronto, Ontario.
Published in the United Kingdom by Constable and Company, Ltd., 10 Orange Street, London WC 2.

This Dover edition, first published in 1975, is an unabridged republication of the work first published in 1959. It is reprinted by special arrangement with the original publisher, Mills & Boon, Ltd., 17-19 Foley Street, London, WIa, IDR, England.

International Standard Book Number: 0-486-22724-3
Library of Congress Catalog Card Number: 74-27568

Manufactured in the United States of America
Dover Publications, Inc.
180 Varick Street
New York, N.Y. 10014

CONTENTS

PLATE 2

LIST OF PLATES

on or
facing
page

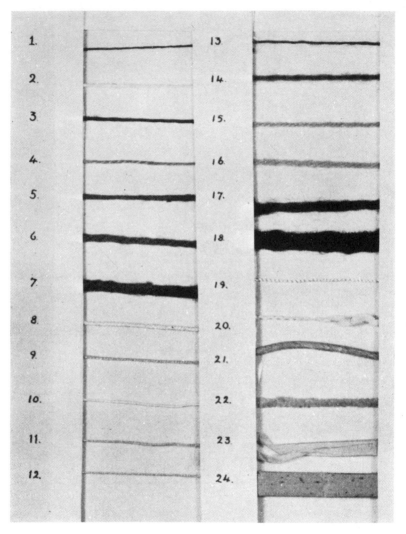

PLATE 3
Key to numbers on pages 39, 40.

INTRODUCTION

W EAVING is one of the crafts which date back hundreds
of years; the horizontal and vertical looms were known
in Graeco-Roman times, the treadle loom was used in New
Testament times.

To-day weaving is highly mechanized, but for the home
weaver simple types of looms are used. Often these are quite
large: some stand over four feet high and are about four feet
six inches in width. These types of looms take up large
amounts of floor space and the noise whilst in action can be
disturbing to other members of a family. They are also expen-
sive to purchase.

The looms mentioned in this book are all smaller ones.
Some of the varieties mentioned can be placed on the lap of
the worker and one can sit by the fireside and weave noiselessly
without disturbing any other member of the family. Working
on such looms one can weave a door mat in the course of an
evening.

I have not attempted in this book to show the reader how
to make long lengths of tweed, which to many people's minds
are boring to make because of the repetitiveness of the work.
To have fun in weaving is to make full use of the wonderful
range of materials which are now available to everyone. By
making articles which are small, one can quickly set up the
looms and weave delightful, original pieces of fabric.

Many children learn simple weaving at school, or may
receive weaving sets as presents. One can have a lot of enjoy-
ment out of the simplest loom, i.e. on a cardboard loom one
can weave the uppers of sandals (such as those shown on
Plate 1), slippers, egg cosies, or gaily coloured mats. Children
aged 7, at their first attempts, can make wonderful mats,
showing a lively sense of colour.

Throughout this book I have tried to illustrate a few of the delightful possibilities which lie in store for those who wish to experiment.

A. V. W.

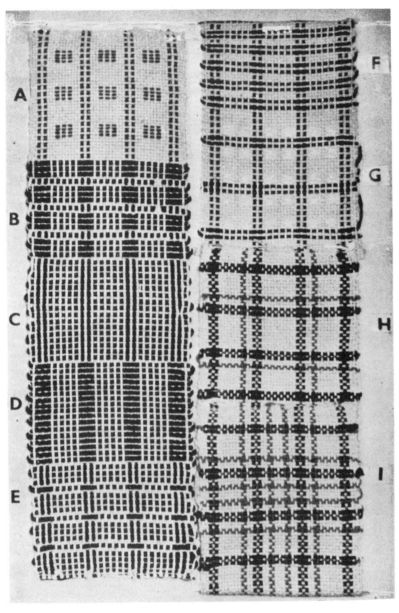

PLATE 4
Key to letters on pages 41–43.

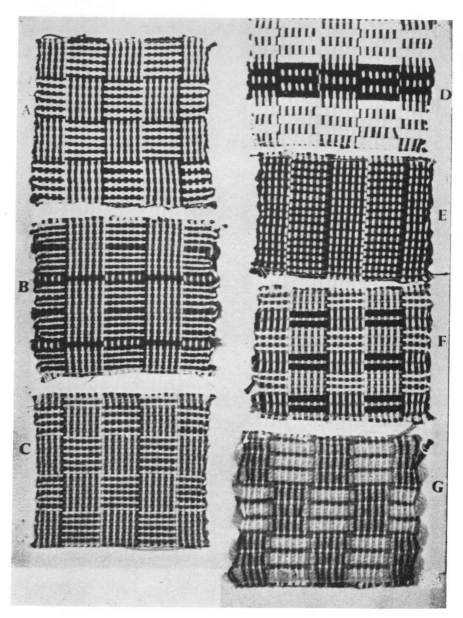

PLATE 5
Key to letters on pages 44, 45.

CHAPTER 1

WEAVING ON CARDS

To produce any piece of woven material one has to have two sets of threads. One set is called the warp and runs lengthwise. These threads must be held taut whilst the weft threads are threaded under and over the warp threads like a web. In order to keep the warp threads taut, it is necessary to stretch them on a frame or loom. The simplest type of frame can be made of stiff cardboard, which has a serrated edge; one can purchase ready prepared cards of various shapes from handicraft stores or one can make one's own.

Cut a piece of stiff cardboard the length of the weaving plus $\frac{1}{2}''$ and the width of the weaving plus 1". Measure down from the top of the cardboard $\frac{1}{4}''$ and rule a line across (Fig. 1), and rule the same depth up from the bottom. Mark the spacing of the warp threads out along this line, $\frac{1}{4}''$ for infants and $\frac{1}{8}''$ for older children. The $\frac{1}{4}''$ mark is very useful for weaving very thick dinner mats, using 2/2s cotton. (For terms describing thicknesses of cotton, see page 39.) Cut from the edge of the cardboard to each mark, thus making a number of snips (Fig. 2). Pass the first warp thread through the first slit and tie the end round the side of the card, take the end of thread and pass through the first slit at the lower edge of card (Fig. 3) and bring up through the second slit, and continue putting on the warp in this way. When completed, secure the last thread to itself as in the beginning.

The weft consists of passing under and over alternate warp threads. For young children or anyone who is doing this for the first time, it is quite fascinating to use short lengths of gay coloured thick wools or cottons. Do not fasten on or

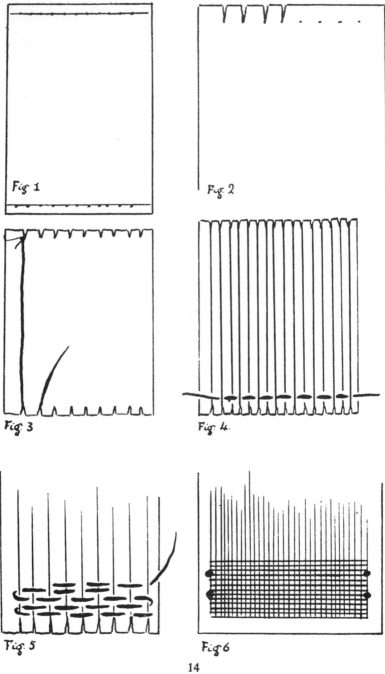

Fig. 1

Fig. 2

Fig. 3

Fig. 4.

Fig. 5

Fig. 6

14

off, but weave across, leaving the ends hanging to form a fringe (Fig. 4). For this type of weaving use coarse wool or cotton. Push down each row close to the previous row so that the warp threads are completely hidden. Continue weaving until the whole of the warp is hidden, then remove the weaving from the cards by slipping the loops of the warp off the cards. If the weaving is to be used for washable mats it would be advisable to machine down the sides of the weaving to make them secure.

Weaving on cards with the sides of the weaving forming selvedges can be obtained by placing the warp threads closer together, i.e. $\frac{1}{8}''$ apart. Start to weave at the lower edge, using a long weaving needle or darning needle. Leave a short end hanging, then pass under and over alternate threads until the row is completed. Now weave back in the opposite direction. Do not pull the weaving tight, otherwise a " waist " will form, with the weaving gradually getting narrower towards the centre and becoming wider again at the opposite end. When joining a fresh length of thread overlap the two pieces for a little way (Fig. 5).

Very attractive designs can be woven on cards. The design may be made by using a warp of different colours and weaving across in the same colours as the warp. The smallest mat in Plate 2 was woven from the chart in Fig. 7 (page 16). When doing the zig-zag design a row of tabby (working over and under alternate threads) should be woven between each row of the pattern, thus preventing any of the warp threads from " floating ", i.e. not being incorporated into the weaving pattern for several rows. The design on Fig. 7 could be used for rug weaving or many of the designs in the pattern darning section could be carried out upon a warp on a card.

When weaving mats on cards it is advisable to rule two lines to join the two rows of serrations; one line at the beginning and the other at the end. If the cards are very thick, drawing pins may be pushed through the weaving into the cardboard; thus the width of the weaving can be held in place as one proceeds (Fig. 6). If there is to be a fringe at the ends of the mats, this must be allowed for when deciding upon the size of the card. A certain area of the warp must be left plain for a fringe, and this can be done by inserting thin cardboard between the warp threads; the depth of the card should be equal to that of the fringe.

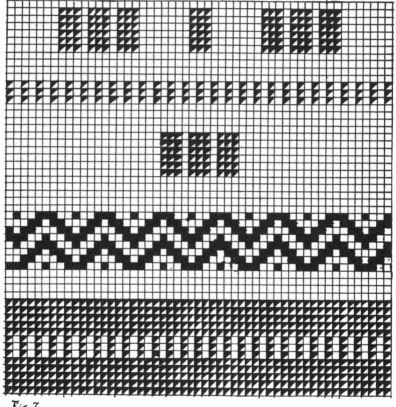

Fig. 7.

So far all the weaving on the cards has been to form oblong pieces of material which can be made up into various useful articles according to the size of the weaving. The articles can be comb cases, pencil cases, marble-bags, purses, ties, etc.

Shaped Cards. These are useful for the making of articles such as slippers, tea cosies, egg cosies, sandals, bags, etc. Again, the shaped cards can be purchased or made from stiff cardboard. When weaving a bag, the warp for both halves may be put on at one and the same time. In addition to the cardboard you will need two brass rings, about $\frac{3}{4}''$ in diameter.

First of all draw out the shape of the bag onto the card. Mark out the spacing of the warp threads carefully, never greater than $\frac{1}{4}''$ apart (Fig. 8). Pierce through each point with a needle so that the position of the warp shows on both sides of the card. The top of each ring can be tied to the cardboard.

Start by tying on the warp thread to one of the rings, pass the thread through the first hole and through the same ring on the outside of the card, bring the thread back through the next hole, then pass through the ring (Fig. 9). Repeat this until all the warp threads are on the card. Draw a line along the first and last warp threads. This is to act as a guide to enable one to see the real shape. Weave in the weft in the usual way, keeping each row close to the brass ring. Do not pull the warp tight because it will pull the bag out of shape.

Continue weaving until the warp threads are completely hidden. It will be necessary to omit some of the warp strands as the sides will gradually become completed before the lower edge of the bag. Weave the second side in the same way. When completed, tear the cardboard close to the holes made by the warp threads, cut the thread holding the rings in position, then remove the cardboard from the bag. It may be necessary to weave three or four extra rows in the space left by the card.

Blanket stitch round the edge of the rings. A handle of twisted threads may be attached to the rings, thus completing the bag. Egg cosies and tea cosies can also be made in the same way (Fig. 10). Sandals may also be made on this type of loom, but only put the warp on one side of the cardboard, and use a linen thread, spacing the warp threads $\frac{1}{4}''$ apart. The weft may be of raffia and candlewick. Decorative patterns may be formed by working in stripes and also passing over

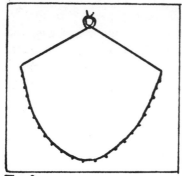

Fig. 8.

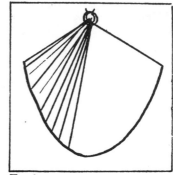

Fig. 9

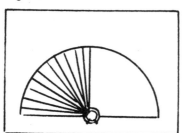

Fig. 10

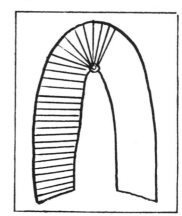

Fig 12

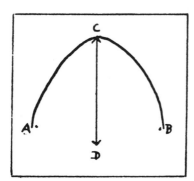

C

A

B

D

Fig. 11

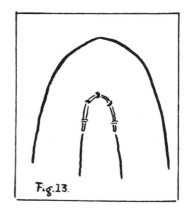

Fig. 13.

several threads at a time. The raffia-soled sandals in Plate 1 were made on this type of loom.

Often it is difficult to do the weaving near to the ring. This can be overcome by passing over three threads and under three to form a pattern, after two or three rows returning to tabby (that is, passing under and over alternate threads).

The plan of the sandal is shown in Fig. 11. From A–B equals the width of the foot, and from C–D equals the length of the front of the sandal. Curve from A to C, then B to C. The sandals may have fronts straight across as in Fig. 10, or may be shaped. The sandal tops may be lined with towelling and the centre ring blanket-stitched to match the towelling. Four more rings, each covered with blanket stitch, may be attached to the inner sole of the sandal; a gay cord can be threaded through the rings and tied round the foot. The soles of the sandals can be of rope, plaited raffia or rubber.

Slippers may be made from odd scraps of gaily-coloured wools. Weaving cards may be purchased ready marked out for the slippers, or they can be made from stiff cardboard. Purchase a pair of soles, fleecy-lined if possible, and use these as a guide to make the cards. Draw the outer edge wider than the soles to give a little fullness for the toes. The warp threads are marked out $\frac{1}{4}''$ apart as in Fig. 12, and a ring is used for the rounded portion of the toe. It is easier if a strong needle is used to pierce through all the marked holes for the warp before actually putting on the warp, which will be straight on the sides, i.e. the warp will go through and back up through the next hole on the card. At the curved part the warp threads on the inner edge of the slipper will pass under and over the ring alternately. The child's slipper in Plate 1 was made in this way.

Instead of a ring a thick piece of string may be attached by several stitches to the inner curved edge as in Fig. 13.

Circular weaving is useful when one wishes to make stands for flower pots, or lunch mats. Draw a circle the size of the mat plus $\frac{1}{2}''$ out of strong cardboard. Draw another circle

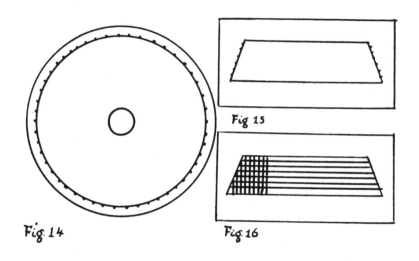

Fig 14

Fig 15

Fig 16

$\frac{1}{4}''$ in from the edge of the outer circle. On this line mark out the position of the warp threads, spacing them $\frac{1}{2}''$ apart and uneven in number. Pierce holes, using a sharp needle, through these marks. In the centre cut out a circle 1″ in diameter (Fig. 14). Tie the end of warp thread to the side of cardboard, then pass the thread through the centre hole and up through one of the pierced holes on the outer ring. Continue winding the warp onto the frame until all the pierced holes have been used. Tie the end temporarily to side of cardboard. Start to weave as near to the centre as possible. Push the rows close together. The weaving may form bands of colour. Do this to both sides. When complete untie the ends of warp and weave into the fabric. Cut away the surplus cardboard close to the weaving. The outer edge may be decorated with a cord or plait.

The sandals (peep-toe) illustrated in Plate 1 were made on a cardboard frame. First mark out the shape of the sandal upper onto a piece of stiff cardboard. Mark out the position of the warp threads $\frac{1}{8}''$ apart, as in Fig. 15. Thread a needle with the warp colour and place on the warp threads by inserting the needle down through one of the holes marked on the cardboard and up through the next mark. The colour of the warp should match the beach bag. The rows of weaving will be quite short to begin with, and gradually become the full width of the warp (Fig. 16). When complete, remove by tearing away the cardboard. The weaving can be backed with sateen or towelling according to the use of sandal. The inner sole can be covered by matching towelling before attaching the upper.

Note. When preparing cardboard for sandals and slippers, always prepare the two at the same time, otherwise two different sizes may be made.

CHAPTER 2

BOX LOOMS AND ROLLER LOOMS

To weave anything of a greater length and a finer weave, it is necessary to be able to raise or lower half of the warp threads at a time; this forms what is known as a "shed", which permits the passing through of a shuttle instead of a needle. To obtain a shed the threads of the warp must pass through the alternate slots and eyes of an instrument called a heddle (Fig. 17). When the heddle is raised or pressed down, half the warp threads will be raised or lowered too. To give room for this up-and-down movement, the warp threads must be held taut across an open space. The simplest method of doing this is to use a box loom.

Box Looms

These can be purchased from handicraft shops, or may be made from an old wooden box, the top and bottom of which should be removed. It is necessary for the sides of the box to be cut down slightly to enable the shuttle to pass through the shed.

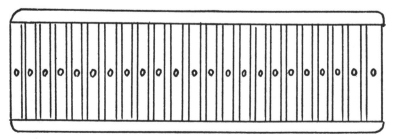

Fig. 17.

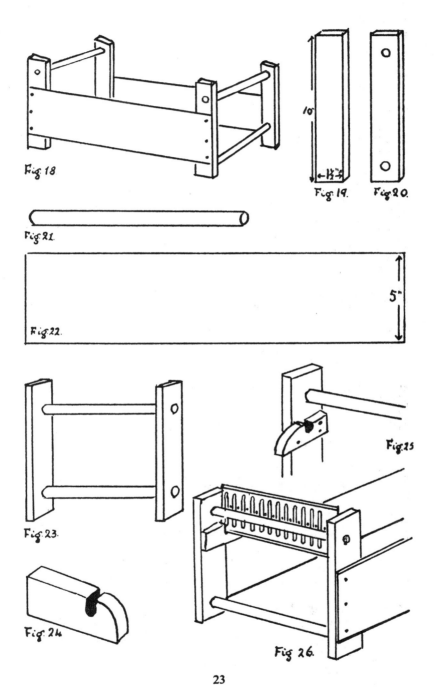

Fig. 18.

Fig. 19.

Fig. 20.

10"

1½"

Fig. 21.

Fig. 22.

5"

Fig. 23.

Fig. 24.

Fig. 25

Fig 26.

Heddles, which can also be obtained from handicraft suppliers, are usually made from metal (chromium plated), having a slot and an eye alternately, and are usually 13 dents to the inch. They can be bought in a variety of sizes varying from 3 to 20 inches in width.

It is possible to make a good loom for very little cost. Wood for the purpose can be obtained from the smaller wood suppliers. If one does not have many tools of one's own, these suppliers will often co-operate considerably when they understand fully what is required of them. It does not take many seconds to drill the holes for dowel rods with the aid of an electric drill.

The loom consists of four wooden uprights, held apart by dowel rod, with two large pieces of wood for the sides (Fig. 18).

To make the loom the following pieces of wood are necessary:
4 pieces of wood $1\frac{1}{2}''\times 10''$ and $\frac{3}{8}''$ thick (Fig. 19).

A hole to equal the width of the dowel rod should be drilled $1\frac{1}{4}''$ from the top of each piece of wood. Another hole should be drilled $1\frac{1}{2}''$ from the bottom of each piece of wood (Fig. 20).

4 pieces of dowel rod $10\frac{1}{2}''$ in length or equal to the width of the heddle plus $1\frac{1}{4}''$, and about $\frac{1}{2}''-\frac{5}{8}''$ in diameter (Fig. 21).

2 pieces of three-ply wood or hardboard are required for the sides of the loom. The length of the wood depends upon the size of loom required. $18''$ is a good average, and the depth of the wood about $5''$ (Fig. 22).

To assemble first remove all rough edges of the wood, then glue the dowel rod into the uprights (Fig. 23). Attach the side pieces to the uprights with screws. To attach the heddle holder (this consists of a piece of wood $3''\times 1''$ with a groove to insert the heddle into (Fig. 24)), measure the depth of the heddle eyes to the lower edge of the metal. Measure this depth from the top dowel rod, and attach the wood for the heddle holder (Fig. 25). Check to make sure that the heddle is in the correct position; the eyes should be in direct line with the top of the dowel rod (Fig. 26). This will facilitate easy setting up of the loom and prevent strain on the threads during use.

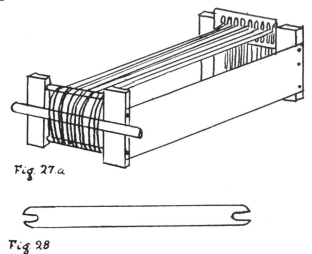

Fig. 27.a

Fig. 28

Setting Up of Warp on a Box Loom

Place the heddle onto the heddle holder on the loom. Pass a thread through an eye on the heddle and round the loom and tie the ends together. This is now one thread of the warp on the loom. Pass a stick under the warp thread. This stick should protrude beyond the edge of the loom (Fig. 27a). The removal of this stick enables the warp to be moved round the loom. Continue putting on the warp, passing the thread alternately through a slit and a hole on the heddle and round the loom, and tie. A reed hook (Fig. 39, page 31) may be found helpful for passing threads through the heddle.

Note. Try tying all threads to a knitting needle or piece of round wood. This enables all the warp threads to be moved evenly at one pull when the warp is moved round the loom.

Before starting to weave, raise the heddle, thus raising the threads that pass through the hole. Into the space thus formed (the shed) insert a flat piece of wood (shed stick) or thin cardboard, which should rest against the end of the loom furthest from the heddle (Fig. 27b). The weaving can then be beaten tightly against the card, thus forming a firm edge. If you are weaving a scarf, the cardboard may be equal to the depth of the fringe.

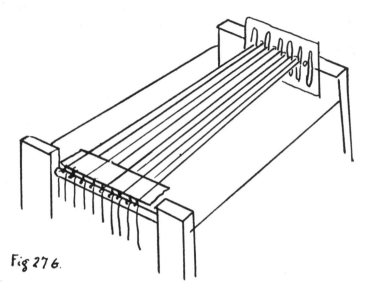

Fig 27 6.

Wind the weft thread evenly on a shuttle. These are long flat pieces of wood with rounded ends and a groove cut in them (Fig. 28). If more than one colour is to be used in the weft, wind the necessary colours on to separate shuttles.

To Weave

Lift the heddle off its rest on the loom and then press it downwards; this gives a gap between the two rows of threads. Pass the shuttle through, leaving 1″ end of the thread free of the warp. Twist this end around the outermost warp thread and leave the end lying along the inside of the shed. Bring the heddle towards you, at the same time pressing the first row of weaving up against the cardboard. This action is generally spoken of as " beating ". Move the heddle back a little way and raise it to make the next shed. Pass the shuttle through.

Do not pull it tight.   Then beat this row close to the previous one.   Continue weaving by raising and lowering the heddle with one hand and passing the shuttle through with the other. Try to keep the width of the fabric even—it is very easy for the beginner to pull the weft too tight.   This type of weaving is known as tabby, i.e. always alternate threads are passed under and over.

As the weaving progresses and nears the opposite end of the loom, the shed becomes less visible.   Now is the time to wind on more of the warp.   First remove the stick which was passed under the warp threads.   Now take hold of all the warp strands firmly and pull towards the underside of the loom.   If a strong knitting needle was attached to the warp during the tying-on stage, pull the needle and all the warp threads will move together.   When the warp threads have been moved round sufficiently, replace the thick stick under the warp to give it a better tension.   If the warp is very slack (this sometimes happens during the course of the weaving) then insert another piece of wood.

Sometimes a warp thread breaks.   If this happens, tie a new length to the broken thread, as far as possible towards the back of the loom.   Thread the new thread through the correct position on the heddle and secure to the fabric by winding the end round a pin.   Make sure the tension is even. Continue weaving, and when complete darn in the loose end.

Attractive scarves can be woven from a selection of odd bits of wool.   If one has several odd balls of wool, together with a neutral colour such as fawn or grey, attractive warps can be set up.   It is advisable to begin at the centre of the heddle and thread onto the loom several lengths of one colour. Make sure that the number of threads are equally spaced on both sides of the centre mark.

Fig. 28b

The above chart indicates a possible threading draft using

four colours in the warp; each square represents two threads. The weft may be woven in the same colours as the warp, or may be woven in one colour only.

The warps for scarves on this type of loom should be of 3-ply wool.   Finer wools are liable to wear and break quickly. A few rows of angora in a weft can make an attractive texture to a scarf as well as form a weft striped pattern.   Many attractive designs can be achieved from a coloured warp, as the plates in this book illustrate.

Roller Looms

The weaving accomplished upon cards and the box loom has always been restricted in length according to the size of card or box.   To weave longer lengths it is necessary to have some method upon which a longer length of warp can be stored ready for weaving.

Roller looms can be purchased from the handicraft suppliers. One of the most useful sizes of loom is a 14″ × 18″ roller variety, especially if it is a shallow one.   From this size of loom one can weave scarves, table mats, runners, bags, etc., door mats and individual pads for a staircase.   This type of loom can quite easily be balanced upon one's lap, one can weave quite speedily upon it and it takes up very little room in a home.

Or the box loom can be converted into a roller loom.

The sides of the box loom, for this purpose, should be made of wood and not hardboard.   The rollers are pieces of dowel rod with attachments which enable the roller to be adjusted, thus keeping the tension of the warp.   There are various ways of doing this, but first remove the lower pieces of dowel rod. Cut two pieces of dowel rod with the width of the loom plus $\frac{1}{2}$″. Cut four circular discs of plywood, each $1\frac{1}{2}$″ in diameter, and drill a series of holes $\frac{1}{8}$″ in diameter and $\frac{1}{2}$″ apart (Fig. 29) into two of the discs.   Put the rollers into place on the loom and attach a disc with holes in at one end of a roller and a disc without holes at the opposite end.   Attach the discs to the

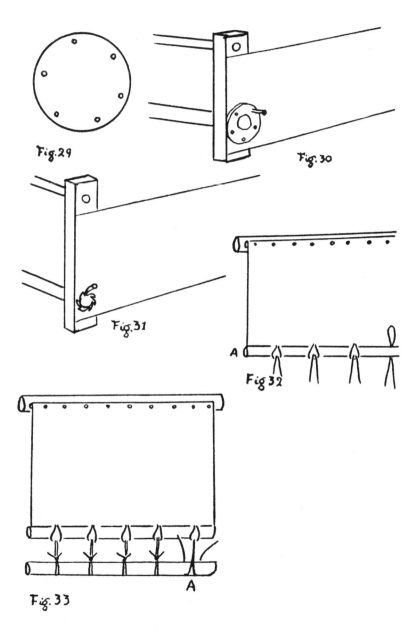

Fig. 29

Fig. 30

Fig. 31

Fig 32

A

Fig. 33

A

dowel with two or three nails. Attach the discs to the other roller. Next drill the holes into the sides of the box to correspond with the holes in the disc. The rollers are prevented from slipping by inserting a nail or peg through a hole in the disc and a hole in the side of the box (Fig. 30).

Another method is to attach a ratchet and pawl to the roller. For this the roller should be $\frac{1}{2}''$ longer than the width of the loom. Remove the lower pieces of dowel rod and insert the new roller. Attach a disc of wood $1\frac{1}{2}''$ in diameter to one end of the roller. At the opposite end attach a small toothed wheel and attach the pawl to the frame. This should be done in such a way that the pawl will fall into a tooth of the ratchet and prevent it from turning (Fig. 31).

To facilitate the tying on of a warp, each roller should be equipped with a piece of calico about $\frac{1}{2}''$ narrower than the width of the roller. Turn under a deep hem and thread a flat piece of wood through this (A, Fig. 32). Turn under a single turning and nail the calico to the roller. Work eyelets $\frac{1}{4}''$ in diameter and about 2" apart just behind the stick and thread pieces of twine through (lower portion of Fig. 32). Attach a further stick to these pieces of twine (Fig. 33). This is for the warp threads to be tied to. The twine is generally taken over the stick and the two ends are brought up on opposite sides of the main piece of twine as in A, Fig. 33. Then the two ends are tied together. This method of tying on enables the knots to be quickly untied when placing on a warp.

It is necessary to prepare the warp for this type of loom and therefore essential that apparatus is used to enable the warp threads to be wound on of an even length. There are various types of apparatus, such as a warping frame, which is a board made to hang upon a wall. The board has a number of pegs upon it, and is suitable for really long lengths of warp. A simpler method is to use pegs which can be clamped to a table or desk. Fig. 34 illustrates one of the inexpensive sets of posts. First of all place the posts the required distance apart, i.e. the length of the warp plus 9" for wastage in tying on for a roller

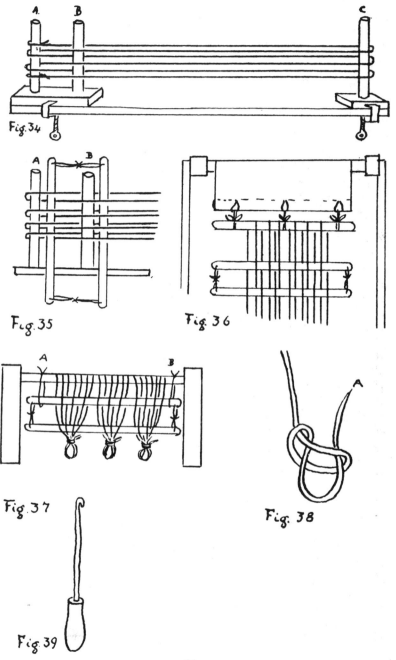

Fig. 34

Fig. 35

Fig. 36

Fig. 37

Fig. 38

Fig. 39

loom, more for the larger looms.   Next count up the number of holes and spaces on the heddle (width of article required). Remember to end up with a hole.   Add two extra at each end, so that the two threads at the beginning and end may be threaded double to make a firmer selvedge.   It is advisable to place the balls of wool or cotton to be used for the warp inside large jars or jugs.   These containers enable the threads to be pulled easily and give a constant flow of thread without the balls getting tangled round furniture.

Tie a loop in the thread and slip it over peg A (Fig. 34). Take the thread in front of peg B and pass it on in front of peg C, and bring it back, passing at the back of peg B.   Then bring the thread to the front and pass in front of peg A and round this peg and in front of peg B.   Continue in this way, always crossing the threads between pegs A and B.   Often it is necessary to join a fresh supply of thread on; always join on at the pegs at either end.

Slip a shed stick (flat piece of wood with a hole in each end) through the warp and alongside peg A (Fig. 35).   Place a second shed stick down the side of peg B.   These two sticks should be tied together at the top and bottom as in Fig. 35. They hold what is termed the cross firmly in position.   This cross keeps the threads separate and prevents them from becoming a tangled mess.

The shed stick which was tied to the back roller (Fig. 33) should be removed, and this stick, which we will call X, is passed down the side of peg A of the warp.   Pass another stick down the side of peg C.   It is usually helpful if two people remove the warp from the warping posts.   One person to hold both ends of the stick which was passed through at peg C, and the other person to hold securely the stick (X) which was passed down the side of peg A.   The warp should now be lifted off the warp pegs and stick X is once again attached to the back roller of the loom as in Fig. 36.   At this stage the warp should be carefully spaced out to the width required. Holding the warp tight, gradually move the cross forward, and wind the warp onto the back roller. During the winding on of the warp, flat sticks (warp sticks) should be placed between the warp and the roller at intervals, or place sheets of clean paper between the roller and the warp. This is to prevent the layers of the warp from becoming intermingled.

When the cross sticks are within about 15" of the end of the warp, tie one of the cross sticks to the back of the loom as indicated by A and B in Fig. 37. Cut the ends of the warp loops, then tie the threads into groups, using a slip knot. Thus a pull on the loop end A (Fig. 38) enables the group of threads to be quickly untied. Next pass the threads through the heddle. It is often easiest to commence to thread from the centre of the heddle outwards. Use a reed hook (Fig. 39) to thread with.

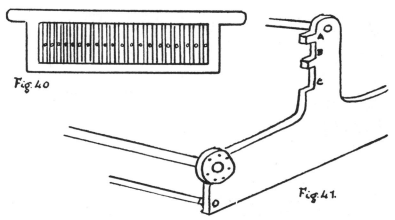

Fig. 40

Fig. 41.

The heddles which are supplied with roller looms are generally built into a wooden frame as in Fig. 40. The protruding pieces of wood fit onto the shaped sides of the loom (Fig. 41). When the heddle is raised to form the shed, it rests on point A. The neutral point is point B, and the lower shed is marked by the letter C in the diagram. When threading the heddle in this type of loom, tie it in the neutral position.

There are various ways of putting on warps, some of which require more equipment. Throughout this book I have tried to minimize the equipment required to enable simple weaving to be carried out both in the house and school.

Improvisation of warping equipment can be carried out in the home by using chairs. If dining chairs are turned upside down on a table then the legs may be used as a warping frame. Place the chairs close together so that they do not slide about. A book or box could be placed on the table to prevent two chairs touching, and the legs of these two chairs will be spaced slightly apart. The leg of one chair could be used as peg A, and the leg of the next chair represent peg B. Carefully measure out the length of the warp, using a tape measure, and commencing at peg A gradually measure the length of the warp, measuring round the chair legs.

Calculations of Warps

The number of threads in a warp depends upon the width of the article and the number of dents to the inch. To calculate for a scarf 9″ wide, and with a finished length of 50″:

No. of dents to 1″ = 12
Width of weaving = 9 × 12 (dents per inch) = 108
Thread the first 2 dents and last 2 dents double to
    make a firm edge   4

                               Total   112 threads

Length of warp = length of article plus 15″ waste.
Therefore length of scarf = 50 + 15″ waste = 65″.

Mats and cushions or any article which has a fringe—an allowance must be made when calculating the warp.

Instructions for making some simple articles, the material for which can be woven on these looms, are given in Chapter 7.

CHAPTER 3

WEAVING MATERIALS

THERE is a wonderful range of materials, both natural and man-made fibres, which can be used for weaving. The choice of the materials depends upon the article being made— Is it something to be worn next to the skin? If so it must be soft to touch; it might be made from wool or nylon. Is it to be hard-wearing such as a floor covering? Then it can be woven with rug wool, strips of rags or strips of plastic, and if a rough surface, then plaited rushes, sea grass or coarse string. Remember that the warp threads, i.e. the threads which run from the front to the back of the loom, should always be the stronger threads because they get the most strain during the actual weaving.

Cottons

When using the finer ones such as 12/2s, 12/3s, 10/4s on a 12 dent reed, use them double for the warp. They may be used single for the weft, double or plied. (See page 38 for an explanation of these terms.)

Cotton of the 6/2s and 2/2s types may be used for the warp, also for the weft. The thicker cottons, 4/4s and candlewick, are only suitable for the weft, and look best when only a small amount is used in conjunction with the finer threads.

All the above are suitable for cushions, mats, bags, etc.

Linen threads are used for table linen and are sometimes mixed with other yarns; usually the warp would be of linen. The D.M.C. No. 6 Flax lace thread can be used singly and No. 12 and No. 16 used double. These threads are sold by the skein.

Wool. The 3-ply and 4-ply are best for warps on the rigid heddle used on box and roller looms. The finer threads may be used on the 4-way looms. The 3- or 2-ply may be used for the weft. These are suitable for scarves. Wool may also be used in conjunction with a cotton warp and often the quick-knit and 4-ply wools help to give added interest to the texture.

Rayon should only be used for the weft and, again, is best used with other threads.

Angora is a form of very soft wool and is only suitable for the weft. May be used in a scarf, or a few rows in evening bags gives a pleasant texture.

Nylon. There is a wide range; only use the variety about the thickness of 2-ply wool for the warp. There is a wonderful thick, soft variety which is very suitable for scarves or to give a pile texture to cushions.

Lurex. A brilliant metallic thread which can be purchased in a wide range of colours. Is unsuitable for a warp, but delightful if used sparingly in a weft for stoles, evening bags and some cushions.

Chenille is a delightful fur-like thread suitable for a warp when a pile effect is required.

Gimps may be made of cotton or wool. They are finely spun, with regular pieces which are loosely spun, suitable for cushions, mats, bags, etc.

Piping Cord makes a distinctive ridge pattern if combined with finer threads in a weft. Always boil before using. It is sold in various thicknesses, varying from 1d. to 2½d. a yard.

Raffia is suitable only for a weft, and should be soaked before using to make it more pliable. Looks best when a group of warp threads are placed close together and then a gap left before the next group of warp threads.

Rushes. Soak overnight before using, then squeeze each

reed separately to remove moisture, and wrap in a damp cloth. Use whilst still damp. If being used for mats or hangings, cut the rushes the width of the warp plus 1". This enables them to be more easily handled. If using the rushes for floor coverings, prepare as before but plait three rushes together to be used as a weft thread; the plaiting makes them stronger.

Rushes, which can be purchased by the bolt though this is rather a large quantity, can be collected from the countryside in June and dried, preferably under the roof of a shed so that the air can get at them.

Cane. There are various varieties of cane which are suitable for weaving flat articles such as mats or hangings. The glossy flat seating cane obtainable in a variety of widths makes an attractive surface. Cut the canes the width of warp plus 1" extra and soak for about 15 minutes. When using cane in the weft, always weave one length of some other kind of thread between each piece of cane.

Sea Grass. This is very tough and coarse and is therefore only suitable for floor coverings.

String is obtainable in a variety of thicknesses; the finer ones are suitable for warps and the very coarse variety may also be used for weaving.

Rug Wool. There are two thicknesses: one is thick, the other thin. Both are suitable for the weft of floor coverings, but the thick is more suitable for tufts.

Plastic is suitable for floor coverings. Often old macs can be used for this purpose, or worn-out plastic aprons. It is necessary to have a few so that one can weave in bands of colour. Always warm the plastic before using—it becomes more pliable. Cut into 1" wide strips.

Grasses and Straw. Many of the coarse varieties of grass which are found in the countryside may be used for weaving, also straw which has a soft golden colour.

Cellophane can be purchased in bundles already cut to a width of 1″. It is suitable for straight hangings and looks best on a spaced warp, i.e. a group of warp threads threaded close together and then a large gap left before the next group is threaded.

Fleece. This may be sold by weight or collected from the hedgerows and spun and dyed by vegetable dyes. For those who are interested in this aspect of weaving there are numerous books or leaflets on the subject.

Plying. This is the term used when more than one thread is twisted together. This is often necessary when a thicker thread is required for a weft pattern. When a thread of some 5 or 6 feet is required, this can often be done by oneself. Pass the end of the thread round the knob or handle of a door and walk to the far end of the room, slowly unwinding the ball with one hand and pulling the end which has been passed through the handle. When the two ends are about 10–12 feet away from the door, cut off the thread and twist the two ends together. When it looks well twisted keep the two ends securely in the right hand and, passing the left hand down the thread towards the centre, walk to the door. Slip off the loop of thread and place alongside the ends held in the right hand, and knot together. Shake the whole length vigorously so that it twists together, then hold up as high as possible to complete the twisting process. You now have *a 4-ply thread or cord.*

Calculating Quantities of Materials

Wool is generally spoken of as being of such and such a ply. This means the number of bends or folds; therefore 2-ply wool has two folds or two strands twisted together. The greater the number of strands, the less yards to the ounce.

```
2-ply wool has 240–280 yards per oz. (approx.)
3-ply  ,,    ,,  165–180   ,,    ,, ,,      ,,
4-ply  ,,    ,,   50–70    ,,    ,, ,,      ,,
```

Cotton. You will have noticed that one speaks of cotton as a number with a dash, then another number. This is obtained from the system of counts used in cotton. A hank contains 840 yards, and the number of hanks to the pound represents the count. If there are 16 hanks (each 840 yds.) in 1 lb. the count is 16s, meaning 16 hanks = 1 lb.

The yarn is generally composed of more than one thread. The number of threads twisted together is always indicated by the side of the count. If one sees "4/16s", this means that 4 threads are plied together, reducing the number of hanks to 4 per lb. Some catalogues will indicate the number of yards to the ounce or pound.

To calculate the weaving materials required for any article carry out the following:

Multiply the width of the article by the number of threads per inch, then multiply this by the length of the warp.

Therefore a warp 9″ wide, with 13 threads to the inch and 2 yards in length (9 × 13 × 2) = 234 yards. Approximately the same quantity is required for the weft. Therefore the total amount would be 468 yards. If three-ply wool were being used, divide 468 by 165 (number of yards per oz.) and approximately 3 oz. would be required.

Types of Threads used in Weaving (Illustrated in Plate 3)

1. 12/2 mercerized cotton   4. 6/2 mercerized cotton
2. 12/3 plain cotton   5. 2/2 cotton
3. 10/4 plain cotton   6. 4/4 plain cotton
                7. Candlewick cotton

8. D.M.C. No. 6—16 yards per skein ⎫
9. D.M.C. No. 12—27   „   „   „   ⎪
10. D.M.C. No. 16—40   „   „   „   ⎬ D.M.C. Flax lace
11. D.M.C. No. 20—45   „   „   „   ⎪   threads
12. D.M.C. No. 40—51   „   „   „   ⎭

13. 1-ply wool   15. 3-ply wool
14. 2-ply wool   16. 4-ply wool

17. Quick-knit wool
18. Rug wool
19. Rayon
20. Gimp
21. String
22. Chenille
23. Raffia
24. Rushes

CHAPTER 4

WEAVING DESIGNS

THIS chapter is devoted to some of the interesting patterns and textures which can be achieved on the very simple box or roller loom. The threading drafts are given on squared paper; each square represents either a hole or a slit on the metal heddle. The colour of the thread is indicated by the different marking in the squares. When darning patterns into the warp it is best to have a perfectly plain-coloured warp so that the weft colours show up very clearly.

There is mention in this chapter of the use of a four-shaft loom for close weaving of rushes, cane, etc. More details about four-shaft looms will be found in chapter 6.

Many variations of pattern can be obtained from the same warp. In the first seven patterns shown on Plate 4, the warp consists of black and yellow, 13/3s cotton, used double. The crosses in the threading draft (Fig. 56) represent the black threads, the dots are yellow.

Fig. 56

A. The weft is all yellow with a pattern carried out in green. The pattern threads were first picked up by a ruler, which is turned onto its edge, thus forming a shed through which the shuttle is passed. In this example the ruler picked up three alternate threads in the centre of each stripe. The ruler is placed at the back of the heddle and the threads picked up must be those which pass through the slits in the heddle, otherwise it will not function to give a shed. When obtaining patterns with the above method, often several threads have to be passed over, and this leaves large loops of thread not caught up in the warp. These loops represent the wrong side of the weaving; thus articles woven from this pattern method should be cushions, stool tops, mats, etc., where only one side of the weaving shows.

B. This warp design was obtained by using 4-ply wool (black) double, then 1 row of 13/3s yellow. These two rows are repeated three times, then 2 rows of yellow, 1 row black, 2 rows yellow. Then repeat the black row, yellow row, 3 times, thus forming the pattern.

C. This attractive stripe pattern is formed by using 4-ply black wool double, then one row of 13/3s yellow. D is the reverse side of the weaving of C.

E—is the reverse side of pattern B.

F. This weft pattern is obtained by weaving 1 row black, 1 row yellow, 1 row black, 3 rows yellow.

G. This weft pattern consists of rows of weaving in the same colour order as the warp. The white squares are a darning pattern inserted in between the weft during the process of weaving. The white consists of passing over 3 threads and under 3, then over 3 threads, then behind 5 threads. These include the black warp threads. Three rows are worked (with a yellow tabby row between each row of white pattern). This design would make attractive cushions or stool tops.

H. Red and white have been introduced into the warp to give more colour and the weft is woven in the same colour order as the warp. The white threads in the draft are indicated by solid squares, and the red threads by squares which are half shaded in (Fig. 57).

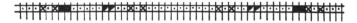

Fig. 57

I. Again another colour arrangement of the warp as the

threading draft indicates. Weave across in the same colour order as the warp (Fig. 58).

Fig. 58

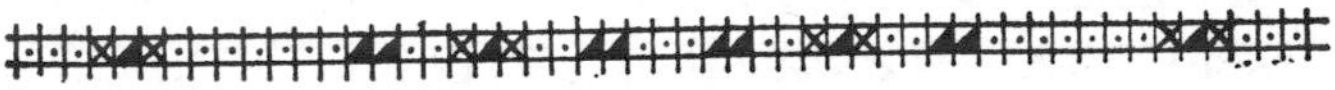

The above two patterns give a little idea of the patterns which can be obtained from weft colour patterns combined with the warp. The bucket bag in Plate 2 was made from a blue and white 2/2s cotton warp. The crosses in the chart indicate the white threads and the dots are the blue ones (Fig. 59).

Fig. 59

The stripe effect is obtained by weaving 3 rows of acid yellow 2/2s cotton and 1 row of raffia; this forms the main part of the bag. The design near the base is obtained by working alternate rows of acid yellow and blue; the larger portion of the border consists of alternate rows of raffia and blue 2/2s cotton.

Basket Pattern and Variations

A basket pattern warp offers great scope for the weaving to show interesting colour reactions. The warp consists of an equal number of light and dark colours, i.e. a red and white or black and white—the greater the contrast in colour the better. The beach bag in Plate 1 was made on a red and white cotton warp and the threading draft is given in Fig. 60. It will be

Fig. 60

noticed that there are two of the same warp colours side by side at regular intervals. The weft consists of rows of various thicknesses, and eleven rows constitute the pattern. They are:

1 row white 1-ply; 3 rows yellow 2-ply; 1 row white 1-ply;

1 row black candlewick cotton; 2 rows green 2-ply; 1 row white 1-ply; 2 rows green 2-ply.

The sling bag in Plate 2 is another example of the use of basket weave. The warp is of 2/2s cotton. The crosses in the threading plan (Fig. 61) indicate the white threads and the dots are the red threads.

Fig. 61

The weft consists of:

1 row black 4-ply wool used double; 2 rows of thin red; 1 row of green candlewick; 2 rows of thin red; 1 row of black 4-ply wool used double; 1 row of yellow 10/4s cotton and 1 row of thin red through the same shed; another row of yellow 10/4s cotton with a row of thin red through the same shed; 1 row of thin red; 1 row of thin red and 1 row of yellow 10/4s cotton through the same shed; 1 row of thin red and 1 row of yellow 10/4s cotton through the same shed. These 12 rows form the pattern.

Plate 5.   These patterns are carried out on a black and white (cotton 13/3s threaded double) warp thread in basket weave.

A. Weft in black and white basket pattern, i.e. weave in the same colour order as threaded.

B. Weft of green, yellow and red.   Weave 8 rows of yellow and green alternately, then 1 row of thick red, and begin to weave again with the same colour as was used before the red was inserted.

C. Weft in blue and yellow, weave in alternate colours for 9 rows, then weave 2 rows of yellow, then another 9 rows.

D. The weft consists of 1 row of double 2/2s white cotton, then a second row is worked in the same shed.   It is advisable to pass the weft thread round a warp thread to lock it.   Change the shed and work another 2 rows of white.   After 5 rows have been worked it will be noticed that an interesting pattern is formed.   The next part of the pattern consists of 5 rows of thick brown wool.   These rows constitute the pattern.

E. Red and black weft worked alternately forms an interesting striped pattern.

F. Weft of blue, yellow and black. Work 7 rows of blue and yellow alternately. Then 1 row of thick black; 1 of blue; then thick black. These rows constitute the pattern.

G. For another interesting pattern use the same type of basket weave threading, only this time insert 2 blue threads at regular intervals to give the change of pattern. Fig. 62 shows the colour chart for threading; the dots represent the blue threads.

Fig. 62

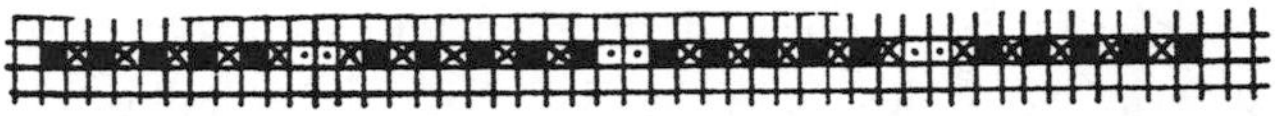

The design at G is worked on the above colour warp. The weft consists of 4 strands of soft 4-ply fawn wool being passed through the shed; make sure that all the threads are flat. Change the shed and weave 1 row of blue. Change the shed and weave 4 strands of 4-ply wool. Do this until there are 3 broad stripes of the fawn wool. Weave 2 rows of blue, then back to the 4-ply wool. Continue until there are 3 broad stripes of fawn and then work 2 rows of blue. The above constitutes the pattern, which can now be repeated from the beginning.

It will be found very interesting to set up a warp based on basket weave and experiment with it, using a variety of coloured threads of various thicknesses.

Plate 6 is a further example of the varied effects that can be obtained by very simple means. The colours used here were blue and white, with lines of thick black worked in between each change of pattern. In the strip of weaving to the left of the picture, the warp was 1 thread white, 2 threads blue, and the wefts were:

(a) all blue   (d) 1 white, 1 blue
(b) all white   (e) 2 white, 1 blue
(c) 1 blue, 1 white   (f) 2 blue, 1 white

(g) 2 white, 2 blue   (i) 2 blue, 3 white
(h) 3 white, 1 blue   (j) 3 blue, 3 white

In the right-hand strip, the warp was 1 white, 1 blue. Wefts
(a) and (b) were all white and all blue respectively. Then:

(c) 1 blue, 1 white   (g) 2 blue, 2 white
(d) 1 white, 1 blue   (h) 3 blue, 1 white
(e) 2 white, 2 blue   (i) 3 blue, 3 white
(f) 2 blue, 1 white   (j) 3 blue, 1 white

By trying out these wefts on a warp of 3 blue and 1 white,
you can obtain still further variations of pattern. A plain
warp may be decorated in a variety of ways. Plate 7 shows
several examples of a 13/3s warp threaded double.

(A) The weft is 1 row of rayon and 1 row of quick-knit wool.
Here the difference in the thickness of thread forms the pattern.

(B) The weft is of a fine twisted thread and the blocks of
brown are inserted during the weaving. The pattern threads
were first picked up by a ruler which is turned onto its side,
forming a shed through which the shuttle is passed. The
threads picked up should always be at the back of the heddle
and those threads which pass through the slits. The pattern
is formed by working several rows of tabby, then one row of
brown with the ruler turned onto its edge, then tabby and back
again to the brown pattern. When all the weaving is complete,
the large brown loops are cut off, leaving the brown oblongs of
woven threads.

(C) There have been additional colours placed into the warp
and these colours repeated in the weft.

(D) To make mats with fringes on all four sides see page 47.

(E) This is an example of pattern darning and was worked
from Fig. 96.

(F) Here is another example of a pattern obtained with the
aid of a ruler. Groups of soft woollen threads are inserted
under a few warp threads to give a raised effect.

(G) The weft is ordinary with a stripe pattern consisting of
1 row of red cotton; 1 row dark blue; 1 row red.

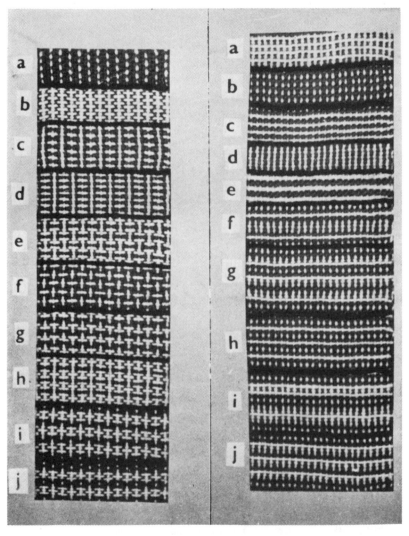

PLATE 6
Key to letters on pages 45, 46.

PLATE 7
Key to letters on pages 46–51.

(H) The inclusion of tufts for decorative purposes is quite useful. See page 51.

(I) Pattern darned onto the warp with the aid of a needle threaded with a thick, coloured cotton.

(J) Looped pattern. See page 49.

(K) Novelty patterns can be carried out with the aid of a needle and thread and working a type of blanket stitch over a group of threads, then carrying on the weaving in the ordinary way. This looks best when a soft wool such as angora is used for the stitching on a fine warp of wool.

(L) What looks like drawn thread work can be carried out by threading a needle with matching weft thread. The needle passes over a group of threads and twists each group before passing on to the next group. Many drawn thread work stitches are quite useful for this type of work.

Warp and Weft Fringed Mats

It is quite simple to weave mats with a fringe of the warp threads and also of the weft, giving a fringe on all four sides (Plate 7,D). Set up the loom in the usual way, then place 4 warp threads about $\frac{3}{4}''$ away from the main warp. This is to allow for the fringe on the sides.

Fig. 63

Fig. 63 illustrates the threading of the heddle and the gap left at the sides for the fringe. The chart illustrates a two-colour warp. Weave right across to the outer warp threads. Do not pull the weft thread tight. Continue for about 4". Then begin to work hemstitch on the sides of the weaving. To do this, thread a needle with matching thread, secure at the lower left-hand edge of the weaving. Pick up a group of threads (about 4) (Fig. 64), pull the needle through and pass it to the back of the weaving and bring through on the right side.

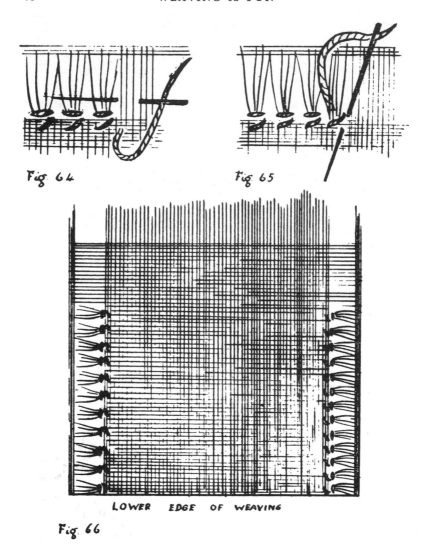

Fig. 64

Fig 65

LOWER EDGE OF WEAVING

Fig 66

Fig. 65—Continue working the hemstitching to within 1″ of the top of the weaving. Work hemstitching on the other selvedge side of the weaving, so that the 2 rows of hemstitching are being worked along the length of the weaving as in Fig. 66. The hemstitching across the mat may be worked whilst the weaving is still on the loom. This should be done after the last row of weaving of each mat. Two strips of cardboard should then be inserted between the warp threads, and these strips of card should equal the depth of the fringe on each mat. Then commence to weave the next mat.

Looped Weaving

A raised pattern can be worked on to a plain background by working looped weaving. Plate 7, J shows a small sample of looped weaving.

The looped pattern is formed by passing the weft thread round a knitting needle or thin rod. First pass the shuttle through the shed, next take a knitting needle, then pick up the weft thread, making the thread wrap round the needle each time it is picked up. If this is done at regular intervals it will form a pattern. Always weave one row of tabby between each row of loops.

A simple method of working the loops can be done by threading a blunt needle with a length of thread (Fig. 67). Pass the needle to the back of the rod or knitting needle (Fig. 68).

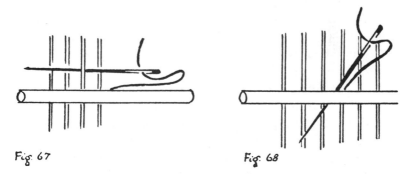

Fig. 67   Fig. 68

This process of Figs. 67 and 68 can be carried out in one movement. Fig. 69 shows the loops formed over the rod.

Another method of working a loop which has the advantage of being able to be cut, thus forming a pile effect, is slightly more complicated because the thread must be more securely

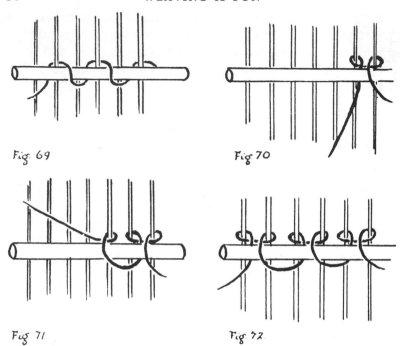

Fig. 69

Fig. 70

Fig. 71

Fig. 72

attached to the warp to prevent it from falling out when cut. Fig. 70 shows the thread being passed round a warp thread from left to right. Pass the thread round the second warp thread in the same way, then under the rod. Fig. 71 shows the thread being brought over the rod and passing round the warp thread. Make sure that the end of thread passes through the loop and then continue passing the thread round the warp threads and over the rod. Weave a row of tabby, then remove the rod and work the next row of loops. When the weaving is complete the loops may be cut to form the pile effect.

The shaded squares on the charts indicate the position of the loops. In Fig. 73a the shaded squares and straight lines indicate the passing of the thread between the rows of loops. Weave a row of tabby, then remove the rod. Fig. 73b shows a chart suitable for a cushion cover. Only one quarter of the design is given in the chart (p. 52).

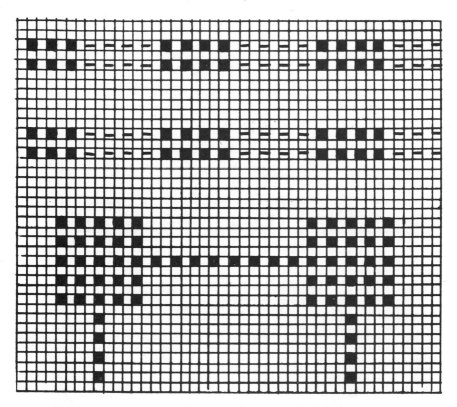

Fig. 73a

Attractive designs can be formed by the working of tufts. These can be worked in rows or in groups to form a pattern (Plate 7, H). The tufts can be made of thick thread or several strands of a finer thread. Cut the tufts at least 3″ in length because if they are too short they are difficult to handle, and after they have been inserted they can always be cut shorter. To make the tufts pass the ends of the tuft round 2 warp threads as in Fig. 74. Pull tight, and after putting in the necessary number of tufts, work rows of tabby until the next tufts are required. This type of tufting is used for the making of rugs.

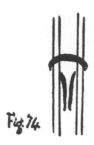

Fig. 74

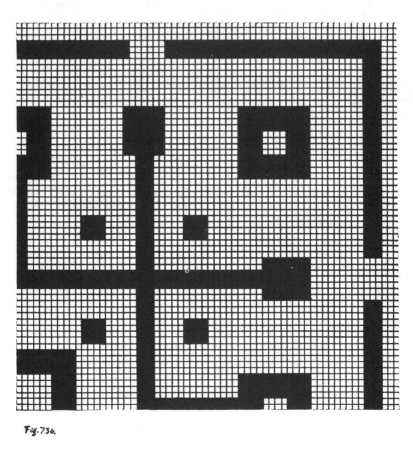

Fig. 73b.

Figs. 75 and 76 show charts with plans suitable for loop weaving.

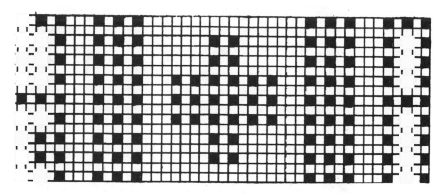

Fig. 75.

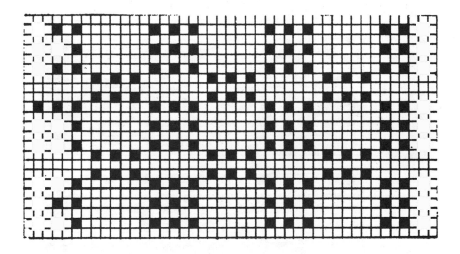

Fig. 76

Further Designs

Attractive designs can be carried out by the arrangement of the warp colour.

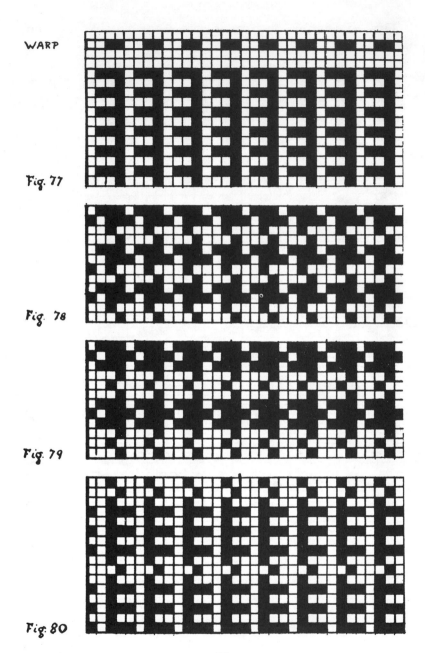

WARP

Fig. 77

Fig. 78

Fig. 79

Fig. 80

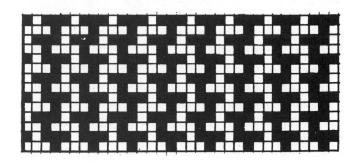

Fig. 81.

Figs. 77–81 show some of the designs which can be carried out on a warp of 2 light and 2 dark threads.

Fig. 77.—The weft consists of 1 row light and 1 row dark.

Fig. 78.—The weft consists of 2 rows light and 2 rows dark.

Fig. 79.—A weft of 3 rows light and 3 rows dark.

Fig. 80.—The weft consists of 3 rows light; 1 row dark; 1row light; 1 row dark; 1 row light; 1 row dark; and then repeat.

Fig. 81.—The weft consists of 1 row dark and 1 row light through the same shed. Change the shed and put across 1 row dark and 1 row light, through the same shed.

Designs carried out on a warp of 4 light and 4 dark threads are shown below and overleaf.

WARP

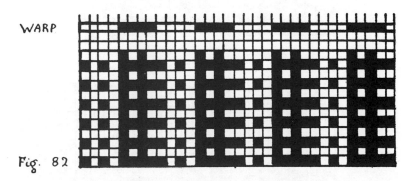

Fig. 82

Fig. 82.—The weft consists of 1 row dark and 1 row light.

Fig. 83—The weft consists of 1 row light and 3 rows dark.

Fig. 84.—The weft consists of 2 rows light worked through the same shed, change the shed and work two rows dark through the same shed.

Fig. 85.—This pattern is formed by working 1 row dark and 1 row light through the same shed. Change the shed; 1 row dark and 1 row light in the same shed.

Another effective variation would be to work two rows in dark and 2 rows in light.

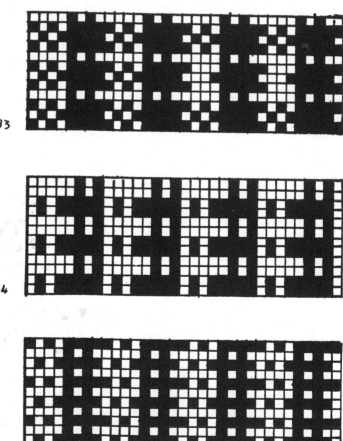

Fig. 83

Fig. 84

Fig. 85.

Scarves can be quickly woven in a delightful range of pattern and colour. The warp can be made up of bands of colour and if they are arranged in a decorative order a striped pattern may be formed during the weaving. The cherry-red and grey scarf illustrated in Plate 2 has a cherry-red warp of 4-ply wool. This is indicated by the black square in the threading chart and the cross indicates the grey threads of 3-ply wool. The C below the end black square indicates the centre of the warp.

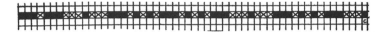

Fig. 86

The weft is of 3-ply cherry wool and 3-ply grey wool. 3 rows red, 1 row grey, 1 row red, 1 row grey, 1 row red, 1 row grey.

These 8 rows form the pattern of the scarf. A change of pattern was made at the lower edge of the scarf. This was obtained by working 4 rows of red instead of 3 rows. The total length of the warp was 63″ and it took 1 oz. of 4-ply and 1 oz. of 3-ply cherry wool, and 1 oz. light grey wool.

The bag with the white cords illustrated in Plate 2 (bottom left-hand corner) is an example of using a spaced warp for threading a cord through the space, thus enabling a bag to be woven quickly and at the same time making the threading space.

The warp was 34″ in length, and consisted of red cotton (x on the chart), white 8/8s cotton (. on the chart), black 12/3s cotton used double (black squares on the chart). Read the chart from left to right and the blank marks on the chart are the spaces left when threading the warp through the heddle.

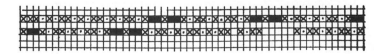

Fig. 87

The weft consists of 2 rows of red quick-knit wool; 1 row yellow 12/3s; 1 row yellow 12/3s used double; then 1 row single; 2 rows red quick-knit; and 1 row of piping cord. These 8 rows form the pattern.

After weaving for 5″ or 6″ it is advisable to thread an embroidery needle with one of the warp coloured threads, and stitch the spaced weft threads in groups, leaving the piping cord free, as the illustration in Fig. 88. shows.

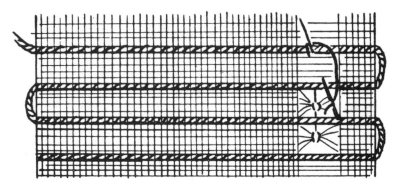

FRONT OF LOOM

Fig. 88

Spaced Warps

When weaving with thick coarse materials such as rushes, cane, raffia, soft thick wool, etc., it is necessary to space the warp to form stripes. Colour can be introduced into the warp to form patterns, see Plate 8. The chart below indicates the placing of the colour of the warp, also the number of dents which are left empty.

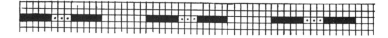

Fig. 89

The illustrations in Plate 8 are as follows:

(a), (b), (c), (d) and (e)—the warp is black (dark squares) 13/2s, used double, and white (dots on chart) 6/2s mercerized cotton.

Wefts

(a) Acid yellow soft thick cotton like 4/4s with natural colour soft untwisted string often used by plumbers for packing pipes.

(b) Medium shade of blue double-knitting wool, used double but not plied together, also acid yellow cotton gimp, and rushes.

(c) Weft of double-knitting wool used double with 13/2s black used double and rushes.

(d) Weft of a novelty twisted white cotton with acid yellow soft thick cotton.

(e) Weft of acid yellow soft thick cotton, with a cream colour thick soft wool, rather like rug wool in thickness but as soft as baby wool.

When using rushes, raffia, cane, etc., if a really high standard of finish is required, it is essential to have the warp threads tightly packed together, often as many as 50 to the inch. This can only be achieved on a 4-shaft loom. It may be a table model, and if the reed is 12 dents to 1″ then thread 4 threads through each dent. If a 24 dents to 1″, thread 2 threads through each dent. For this work the warp must be fine, such as 13/2s cotton plain or mercerized. (f), (g), (h) and (i) in Plate 8 are all woven on a 48 threads to 1″ warp. The space between the grouping of threads can be arranged according to taste.

(f) The warp is alternate threadings of brown and yellow cotton, the weft of raffia and thick soft wool. Raffia bends easily and therefore can be used like an ordinary weaving thread and joined by overlapping.

The warp for the next three examples consists of 13/2s cotton, alternate threading of black and white. The threads are 40 to the inch and this can only be achieved on a 4-shaft loom. Again this is an example of a spaced warp threading.

(g) The weft consists of one row of 13/2s cotton; 1 row white, then 1 row black, 1 row white, then a piece of cane. These 4 rows form part of the design, which is repeated 3 times. The next repeat is formed by weaving alternate rows of 2 thicknesses of 13/2s cotton twisted and doubled (black) and cane.

(h) The weft is made up by weaving three rows of black 13/2s cotton used double, then a piece of rush, these 4 rows form 1 unit of the pattern. The white stripes are made from 2 thicknesses of 13/2s cotton twisted double.

(i) The weft consists of 2 thicknesses of 13/2s cotton (black) twisted and doubled; this is used for all the weaving together with flat pieces of seating cane. The broad pale bands are of flat plaited basket cane.

(j) This example of weaving with raffia was woven on a box loom. The warp consists of 13/3s threaded double, then a gap before the next group of warp threads.

Note: Prepare the cane, raffia and rushes as on pp. 36–7. When the weaving is completed, knot the fringed warp and trim the edges of rushes, cane, etc., even.

Pattern Darning

Pattern making is one of the most interesting parts of weaving. The patterns are usually drafted on squared paper, each square representing a thread of the warp. The designs may form borders or be worked as all-over patterns. This latter method is rather slow. The patterns are worked by threading a blunt-pointed needle with a length of thread. Follow the chart, pass over the correct number of threads, i.e. the shaded squares, and pick up the appropriate number of threads (i.e. the white squares). Follow the chart row for row and between each row of pattern work one row of tabby; this is usually called a binder thread.

There are many attractive designs given in the following charts. They can be used as borders, as shown, and some are also suitable for all-over patterns.

Figs. 89a–d

61

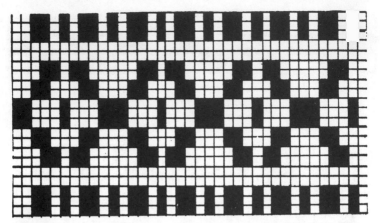

Fig. 90

Fig. 91.

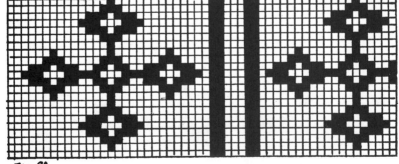

Fig 92

62

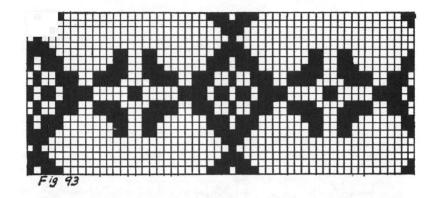

Fig 93

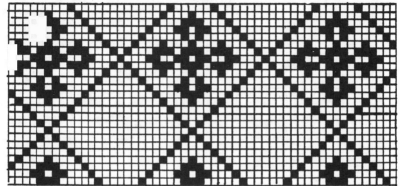

Fig 94

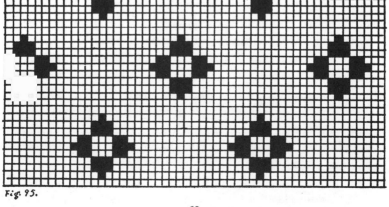

Fig. 95.

63

Many interesting designs can be carried out by using two different coloured threads which partly hide the warp. Fig. 96 shows the chart used for the working of design Plate 7, E. The dark squares represent one colour of thread and the straight lines represent the other colour of thread.

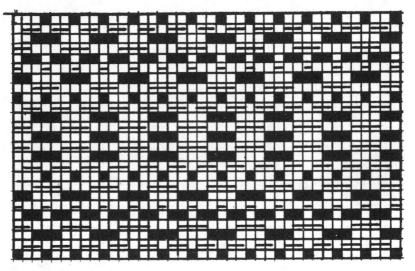

Fig. 96

The designs both for the border and all-over pattern on the small mat illustrated in Plate 2 (top left-hand corner) were worked from the chart at Fig. 97. The warp of the mats was 2/6s fawn threaded double, the weft of black 4-ply wool used double and also woven twice into the same shed. When doing this always loop the weft thread around the first warp thread to prevent pulling out the previous row. Then 1 row of coarse rayon (ecru colour) is woven after each double row of black. The pattern was carried out with thick red cotton. The dinner mat illustrated in Plate 2 (the middle mat of the three) was worked from Fig. 98. The tabby pattern which comes at the beginning of the mat, and which is used between each large design, consists of 1 row pink rayon, 1 row 4-ply black wool

Fig. 97.

double. These 2 rows are worked 3 times. The pattern darning design is worked in turquoise cotton with a row of pink rayon tabby between each row of pattern. The larger design in Fig. 98 is the centre pattern. The mat is completed by working the two previous designs. The design charted in Fig. 99 was used for the mat nearest to the checked bag in Plate 2.

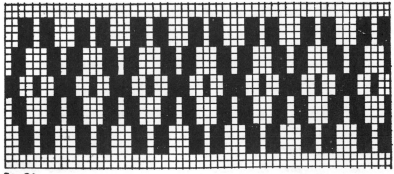

Fig. 99.

(Fig. 98 is overleaf.)

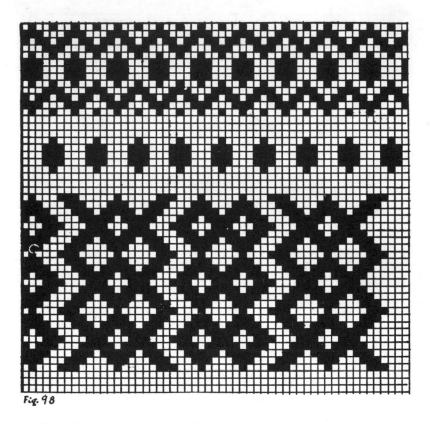

Fig. 98

There are many old traditional patterns which can be used
by this method of pattern darning; one of the simplest patterns
is called Monks Belt (Fig. 100). This design is really based
on two lines of pattern A and B. A is the top line in Fig. 100
and B is the third line. These lines are repeated, i.e. several
rows of A and several rows of B, with tabby (background
colour) worked in between each row. This design can be
developed as in Fig. 101, and may also be used as an all-over
pattern (Fig. 102).

Rosepath is another old traditional pattern. Fig. 103 shows
the basic design and Fig. 104 shows variation of the pattern.
This is a pattern offering many different ideas.

Fig. 100

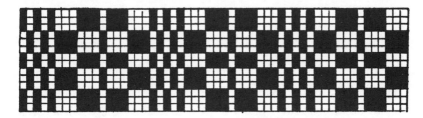

Fig. 101

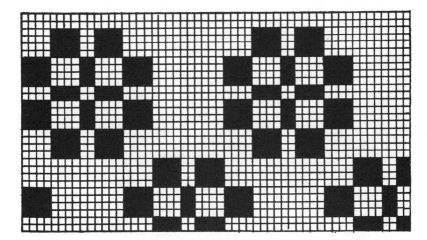

Fig. 102.

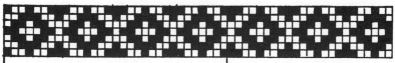

Fig. 103.

Fig. 104.

Pattern Drafting. When one has worked from charts and feels confident about the method of working, one can embark upon the pleasant occupation of drafting one's own original patterns on squared paper. Do not pass over too many threads or go underneath too many as it will weaken the work as well as giving an untidy appearance.

CHAPTER 5

RUG AND TAPESTRY WEAVING

IT is possible to weave small mats for the floor or treads for
a stair.   These can be done on a very simple loom, which
consists of a wooden frame such as a picture frame.   Two
sticks are required to complete the loom.   These sticks should
be equal to the width of the loom, plus 3″, and should be
1″ wide and ½″ thick.   The warp is made of string or linen
threads.   These are wrapped over the frame and tied (Fig. 105).
The stick is then passed through the warp picking up alternate
threads (Fig. 106).   This is done both at the top and bottom
of the loom.

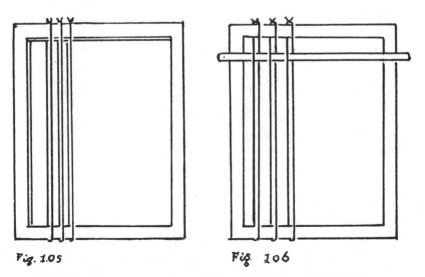

Fig. 105   Fig. 106

An embroidery frame can be used for rug weaving, or the
frame can be made very cheaply (Fig. 107).   The frame really
consists of two long pieces of wood, 1½″ wide, ½″ thick and any

69

length.   These two pieces of wood should have several holes drilled right through them.   These holes should be equally spaced and large enough to take a thick wooden peg (this can be an old meat skewer or dowel rod tapered slightly towards one end).   Two more pieces of wood are required for the top and bottom of the loom.   Two slits should be cut in each piece of wood (as in the lower part of Fig. 107).   This is to enable the uprights to pass through as in the top section of Fig. 107. The holes and pegs are to make the loom adjustable so that various lengths can be woven.

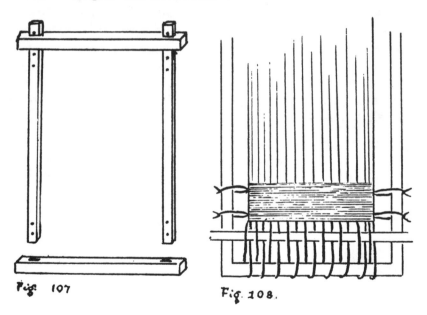

Fig. 107   Fig. 108.

Having placed the warp threads onto the frame, 4 threads to the inch, weave across for about ½″ using thick linen thread or string.   This is to give a foundation for the fringe of the rug.   The actual weaving consists of passing under and over alternate threads, using rug wool.   Do not pull the wool tight, but leave in an arched position, then press down to the lower edge of the loom, using one's fingers, then a coarse metal comb.

Each row must be pushed close to the previous row, completely hiding the warp threads and giving a matt surface. It is necessary to have a strong metal comb to act as a beater. A coarse dog's comb can be purchased at a reasonable cost, or, for very coarse work, a horse comb is quite satisfactory. This type of weaving is known as tapestry.

As the weaving progresses, tie the sides of the rug to the uprights of the loom (Fig. 108). This should be done at 4″ intervals, to keep the mat an even width all the way along. When joining in new lengths of wool, overlap the new end with the old for 3″ to 4″. When joining in lengths of a different colour leave the ends hanging for a few inches on the side nearest the worker. The right side of the rug is on the underside. When completed, the ends can be threaded into a large

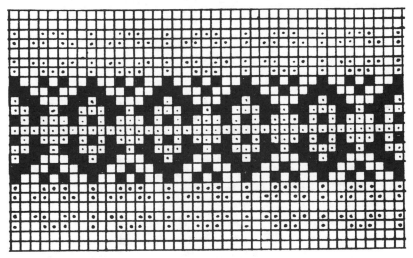

Fig. 109

needle and passed through the loops of weaving, making them secure.

The pattern for mats can be designed upon squared paper, each square representing 1 warp and 4 weft threads. The patterns may have all-over designs or decorative borders

(Fig. 109) or a combination of tufts and ordinary weaving. Charts are given to show a few ideas. Fig. 110 illustrates the chart which was used for a rug carried out in black, grey and green plain weave with tufts of black, grey and red.

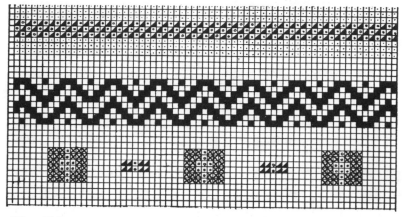

Fig. 110

Squares left blank indicate grey plain weave; those blacked out, green plain weave; those with small dots, black plain weave; larger dots, grey tufts; squares half-blacked, black tufts; crosses, red tufts.

When placing in tufts prepare the wool by first cutting it the required length, i.e. 3″. Pass the wool round 2 warp threads as in Fig. 111. Pull the loop tight. Place in all the tufts, then work a row of tabby. The next row of tufts should be placed around different warp threads and not around the two previously used. Fig. 112 illustrates the appearance on the wrong side of the loops inserted and then a row of tabby. The right side of a tufted rug is uppermost whilst it is being worked. When the whole rug is to be tufted, weave the sides of the rug with a tabby; about 6 warp threads would be sufficient to keep the rug flat whilst in use. An idea for tufted rug is shown in Fig. 113.

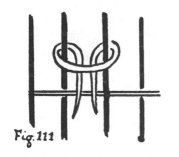

Fig. 111

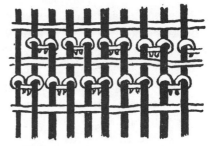

Fig. 112

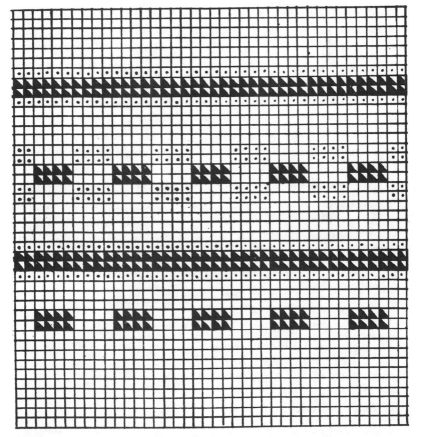

Fig. 113

73

Rugs may also have a looped pattern as well as a flat surface. The loops are made as on pp. 49, 50, only use a thick wooden needle or thin dowel rod so that the loops look in correct proportion to the size of the rug.

Box looms or roller looms can also be used for weaving narrow mats such as door mats or stair pads. Set up the warp using the rigid heddle, but when threading leave spaces so that the threads are 4 to the inch.

Materials for rug weaving can vary, but the actual warp should be of string which is not too thick but firm. Various types of scrap material can be used. Thick woollen materials should be cut $\frac{1}{2}''$ wide. Machine-made knitted garments can, if necessary, be re-dyed and used. These should be cut into $\frac{1}{2}''$ wide strips and cut round and round so that the maximum length can be obtained. Old stockings can be sorted into the various colours and then cut into strips, starting at the top of the stocking. Make full use of the colours for pattern.

Plastic from old aprons, macs, etc., may be cut $\frac{1}{2}''-1''$ wide, and when it is soft and pliable (after it has been placed near a fire) it is quite easy to weave with.

All sorts of mats can be woven from a very wide range of materials, including sea-grass, plaited rushes, coarse soft string.

To complete any type of rug, weave the same number of rows of tabby in string or linen as were worked at the commencement of the rug. Cut the warp threads and knot them in twos or plait in groups. To make the fringe of woollen mats more pronounced, knot oddments of wool in between. This may be done by cutting pieces of wool twice the length of the fringe plus 3". Fold the length of the wool into two, bring the loop through onto the right side of the rug, and just above the linen weaving (Fig. 114). Pass the two ends of wool through the loop (Fig. 115) and pull tight.

Tapestry Weaving

Tapestry weaving has already been mentioned in this section on rug weaving. But finer tapestry work may be carried out

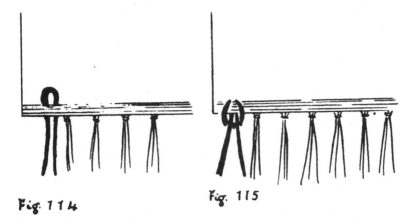

Fig. 114   Fig. 115

and used for stool tops, chair seats, bags or for anything which requires a strong piece of material.

The tapestry weaving consists of spacing the warp threads further apart and using a finer thread than the weft. The work may be carried out upon any type of loom, or a tapestry loom can be made as for the rug loom, page 69, or a picture frame or an embroidery frame may be used. The latter are quite useful for small articles.

The warp is placed onto the frame as for rugs. The number of warp threads to the inch will vary with the type of threads used for the weft, i.e. 12/2s cotton warp with a weft of quick-knit wool or 4-ply knitting wool. The number of threads to the inch could be 6 to 8. The shed for this type of loom may be formed by passing a stick under alternate threads. The other threads may be threaded through loops of thread suspended from a dowel rod (Fig. 116). The loops on the dowel rod may be made of linen thread or fine string. An alternative method of putting on the warp would be to make the loops on the dowel rod first, the number of loops being equal to half the number of warp threads. Place grooved brackets on the sides of the loom for this stick to rest upon (Fig. 117).

Place the warp threads onto the loom so that the alternate threads pass over the shed stick and each thread which passes underneath is threaded through a loop (leash) from the dowel rod.

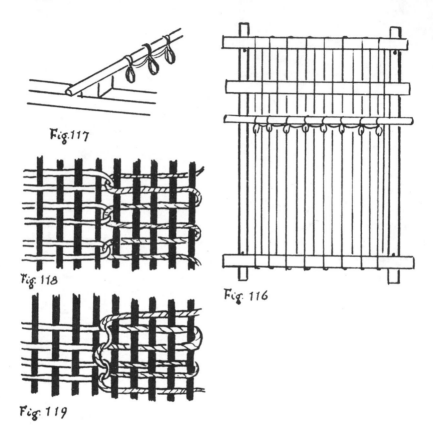

Fig. 117

Fig. 118

Fig. 116

Fig. 119

The shed is obtained by first raising the shed stick onto its side, thus raising half the warp threads, through which a shuttle may pass. The second shed is obtained by raising the rod from which the leashes are suspended.

Place the loom in an upright position and pass the shuttle through the shed. Do not pull the wool tight but leave in a slightly arched position, then press down to the lower edge of the loom, using your fingers or a coarse metal comb. Make the next shed and pass through the shuttle again, leave the wool arched, press down this row close to the first so that no warp threads are visible. Continue weaving in this way and every 4" tie the sides of the weaving to the frame (Fig. 108, page 70) thus preventing pulling in the weaving and making it narrower than the original size.

Patterns in this type of weaving are obtained by using colour in the weft. The patterns may be planned on squared paper (Fig. 107), each square representing one thread of the warp and 2 to 4 rows of weaving, according to the thickness of the weft.

When inserting blocks of colour into the weaving, each colour must pass under and over a certain number of warp threads, according to the design, and then return. This would form a slit in the weaving; to prevent this, each colour must be linked with the adjoining colour before returning, as in Fig. 118 or Fig. 119.

There are special rug looms for larger rugs, but these take up a lot of room in a home.

CHAPTER 6

LOOM DEVELOPMENTS

WITH the rigid heddle variety of loom, one can only lift up or lower the same number of threads, thus always obtaining a tabby weave, i.e. a weave of passing under and over the alternate threads of each row. All enrichment was obtained by using a variety of threads and thus obtaining a change of texture or colour; or by darning patterns into the warp.

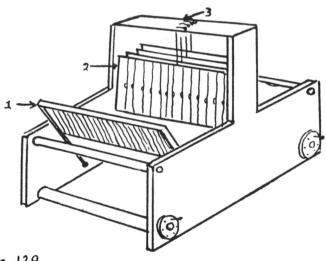

Fig 120

If one removes the rigid heddle and replaces it with a separate shaft for each row of threads (Fig. 120, No. 2), greater variety of pattern can be obtained. This is exactly what has been done with the 4-way loom. Here there are 4 shafts containing a number of eyes made of either twine or metal. When one had the rigid heddles on the loom it was used not only to form a shed for the shuttle to pass through but also as a beater. Now that the rigid heddle has been removed and the shed operation is in the form of raising (Fig. 120, No. 3) the shafts (or lowering them on some types of looms), something must be done to replace the beating operation. This is now done by the reed, which is attached to a specially built frame on the loom (Fig. 120, No. 1).

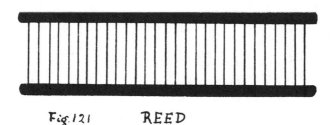

Fig. 121   REED

The reed consists of a series of slits in a frame (Fig. 121) The number of slits to the inch can vary, also the actual width of the heddle. A 12 dents to 1″ heddle is very useful because 2 threads can be put through 1 dent, making it work as if it were 24 dents to 1″. For coarse work the threads may be put through alternate dents; thus the reed can operate as a 6 dents to 1″.

The warp is prepared and attached to the loom as for a roller loom. The threads are first brought through the eyes on the heddles, only this time they will be brought through in a certain order, according to the design of the weaving.

In looking at a pattern design book you will see that the drafts are always carried out on squared paper. Once one can read a threading draft and a tie-up chart, one can pick up weaving books in any language and be able to understand the patterns. The squares are usually in 4 rows, 1 row for each heddle shaft, and the shafts are always numbered from the front of the loom to the back.

In Fig. 122 the right-hand side shows the threading draft for a twill weave.

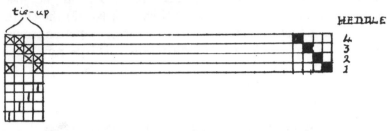

Fig. 122

Read the threading draft from right to left. The first thread of the warp will pass through the eye on shaft 1. The second thread will pass through the eye on shaft 2. The third thread will pass through the eye on the third shaft. The fourth thread will pass through the eye of the fourth heddle. Continue threading in this manner until the last thread is reached. All the threads are brought through the reed and then tied to the front of the loom as for a roller loom.

At the left-hand side of the threading draft is the pick-up or tie-up chart (used for pedal looms). The crosses in the squares indicate which shafts are to be tied to which pedal, or, for table looms, which shafts are to be raised. The strokes in the squares underneath indicate in what order the shafts are to be raised. The first stroke indicates that heddles 1 and 2 are raised. The second stroke indicates that heddles 2 and 3 are raised. The third stroke indicates that heddles 3 and 4 are raised. The fourth stroke indicates that heddles 4 and 1 are raised. These 4 rows form the pattern.

When threading up patterns, always calculate for a selvedge, which is usually 8 threads which are threaded as for twill weave, only put the threads through double.

A much more complicated pattern is shown in Fig. 123. This is not really a difficult pattern and is one of the many traditional ones. It is called Rosepath. The threading chart

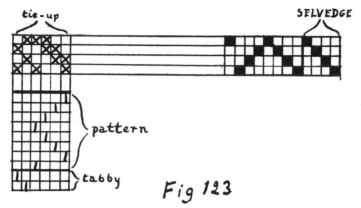

Fig 123

is indicated by the solid squares and the tie-up is on the left. In this particular tie-up the tabby weave is also given. This is shown by the two straight lines on the lower section of the diagram, indicating that heddles 1 and 3 and 2 and 4 are picked up alternately.

There is a great deal of room for experimenting in this section, but I hope that the information given in this brief chapter will enable you to pick up pattern drafts and know what they mean.

In the whole of this section I have always spoken of raising the heddles, but this is not always so. In some looms the shafts are pulled down and not up. Each heddle is attached to the frame of the loom by two springs and the heddle is pulled against these springs. Anyone who is handy with tools can easily convert a roller loom into a 4-shaft variety.

CHAPTER 7

FINISHINGS: AND SOME THINGS
TO MAKE

B EFORE one starts to weave one has already decided what
it is one intends to make. The completing of the weaving
is only one stage on the way to completing the article we have
in mind. Every piece of weaving requires finishing, especially
when oiled wools have been used to weave lengths of tweeds,
travelling rugs, upholstery fabrics, all of which require very
special treatment. But throughout this book the emphasis has
been on the use of various types of weaving yarns other than
wool. After a piece of weaving is removed from a loom it is
generally pressed. If it is wool, use a damp cloth.

Scarf

The ends of a scarf are generally knotted, and this should
be done very carefully, making full use of the warp colours.
One generally takes a group of five or six threads to make
one knot, but if in the warp there were five red threads, then
three grey, it might look best to knot the five red threads
together and then the three grey ones. The knot is formed by
twisting the group of threads carefully together, making a loop
and pulling the ends through the loop. Before pulling the
ends tight, gradually work the loop down close to the weaving
so that after the ends are pulled tight the knot will be right
at the edge of the weaving. Complete all the knots at both
ends of the scarf, then place the end of the scarf out on an
ironing board, comb the fringe gently to make it straight
and press under a damp cloth. If the fringe looks slightly

roughened after pressing, comb again and, using a sharp pair of scissors, cut the fringe level.

Fringe

One of the quickest ways of finishing the edge of a mat is by a fringe. Usually a certain amount of the warp is left unwoven for a fringe, and when this is done the last four rows of weaving must be held secure. This can be done by working a row of hemstitch (see Fig. 64, page 48).

Fringe of Embroidery Threads

Sometimes it may be felt necessary to introduce some of the weft threads into the fringe. Cut the threads twice the length of the fringe plus 1". Thread a needle with a thread of the fringe and insert needle just a few rows above the last row of weaving (Fig. 124a). Leave the end of thread on the right side and bring the needle back up through the hole it entered, leaving a loop on the wrong side (Fig. 124b). Bring the two ends of thread through the loop (Fig. 124c) and pull

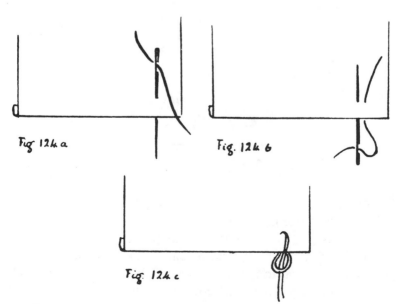

Fig. 124a   Fig. 124b

Fig. 124c

the ends tight. This type of fringe may be put onto articles which have already had a single hem turned up and tacked.

Hemstitch

On some types of mats a neat hem carefully stitched by hemstitch makes a very attractive finish. It is not always necessary to withdraw threads from handweaving to do the hemstitch, as one does from drawn thread work. Turn up a double hem and tack securely in place. Thread a needle with either a matching or contrasting thread of the weaving. Secure the thread in the fold of the hem, and working from left to right pass the needle at the back of a group of threads (Fig. 125a), then into the hem (Fig. 125b). In Fig. 125c is seen a complete row of hemstitch.

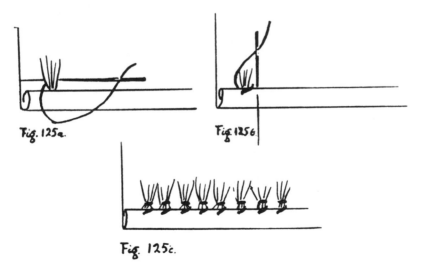

Fig. 125a.

Fig 125b

Fig. 125c.

Pom-poms

These are sometimes used to decorate the tops of slippers, but it is just a matter of taste. Cut two circles of cardboard 2″ in diameter. Cut the centre out of the circles, making a hole of ½″ across as in Fig. 126a. Wind thread or wool through the hole and round the outer edge, passing over the two circles

Fig 126 a.   Fig. 126 b.   Fig. 126 c.

of cardboard as in Fig. 126b. When the small hole in the centre is completely hidden take a pair of sharp, pointed scissors and cut through the outer end of the circle, trying to separate the two discs of cardboard as is seen in Fig. 126c. Slip a piece of thread between the two circles of cardboard and tie tight, then slip off the two circles of cardboard. Trim the pom-pom carefully to make it a good shape.

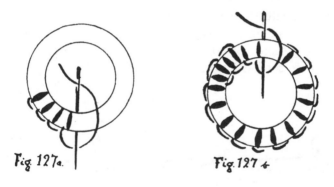

Fig. 127a.   Fig. 127 b.

Rings

Rings are often required for cords to be threaded through for sandals, or may be used on bags for handles. The rings are usually brass curtain rings and the metal is covered with blanket stitch worked in a thread of the warp or weft. Blanket stitch with the loops of the stitches to form the outer edge (Fig. 127a). Then work a second row of blanket stitch in the spaces of the previous row with the loops facing inwards (Fig. 127b).

Cords

These are often required for sandals, handles on bags or for threading through draw bags, for edging cushions or for finishing off various articles. The one great advantage of making one's own cords is that they do match the article because one can always use some of the warp or weft threads.

Twisted Cord

Cut several threads two and a half times the finished length of the cord. Knot the strands together at the ends. Mark the centre of the total length of the threads by tying with a piece of contrasting cotton. Place one knotted end of the thread over a hook, such as a coat hook on a door. Put a pencil through the loop at the opposite end (Fig. 128). Pull the threads taut and turn the pencil to the left, gradually twisting the threads. When fully twisted, take hold of the centre of the cord with the left hand and bend towards the opposite end, which can be removed from the hook and the two ends knotted together. Shake the cord vigorously to give an even twist. This cord is suitable for small articles.

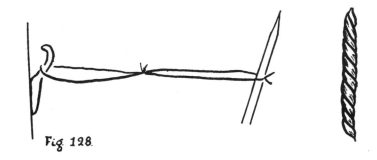

Fig 128.

Three or Four Core Cord

Each group of threads is called a core and the colour of the threads should be divided into the number of cores. Cut each group of threads one and a half times the finished length of cord. Two people must co-operate to make this type of cord, as each core has to be twisted separately. The two people should have sufficient threads to make one core. A should twist her threads in the opposite direction from B. When the threads of this core have been twisted the ends of it should be placed between the knees and held taut whilst the next core is twisted. This process is carried on until all the cores have been twisted; knot the ends together and shake the cord vigorously.

Tassels

These may be placed at the ends of the cords and used on cushions. Cut a piece of cardboard the depth of the tassel required. Using one of the threads used in the cord, wrap

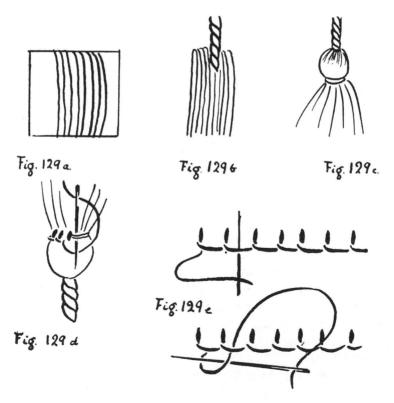

Fig. 129 a.   Fig. 129 b.   Fig. 129 c.

Fig. 129 e.

Fig. 129 d.

round the cardboard many times according to the thickness of the thread, and the thickness of the tassel required (Fig. 129a). Cut through the lower edge of the threads and remove the cardboard. Place the end of the cord inside the tassel section (Fig. 129b).

Stitch through the cord and wrap round the tassel threads to make secure (Fig. 129c). Blanket stitch over the waist thread of the tassel (Fig. 129d). Work trellis stitch (Fig. 129e) into the loops of the previous row of blanket stitching and continue working trellis stitch, decreasing gradually until the cord is reached.

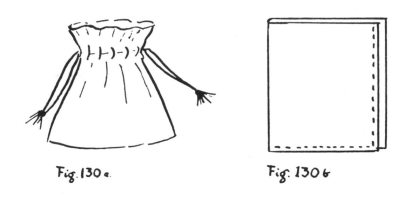

Fig. 130 a.   Fig. 130 b

Bags

Plain simple bags like the one in Fig. 130a consist of an oblong of weaving which has a spaced warp which is used for the cord to be threaded through. Fold the weaving into two so that the one edge protrudes $\frac{1}{2}''$ above the other edge as is shown in Fig. 130b; stitch down one side and across the bottom, then turn under the raw edge of the side and hem down. Turn the bag right side out, thread the cord through the spaced warp and finish off the ends of the cord with tassels.

Note. Before cutting out any shaped article from a hand-woven fabric, it is advisable to machine around the outer edge of the pattern so that there is a row of machine stitching along or around the raw edge; this prevents fraying.

Sewing Bag

A sewing bag with pockets on the side (Fig. 131a) may be made from a strip of woven fabric. (The checked bag in Plate 2 represents the finished article.) The length of the weaving should be equal to the circumference of the bag plus the width of the base of the bag (plus extra for needle and

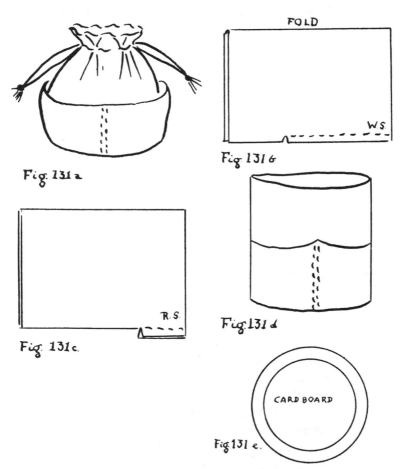

Fig. 131 a

Fig. 131 b

Fig. 131 c.

Fig. 131 d

Fig. 131 e.

scissor case if required). Often the weft pattern can be slightly changed for the making of the small articles. The width of the weaving should be equal to the height of the bag plus the depth of the pockets.

Cut off the strip of weaving for the bag and fold into two. Join the raw edges together by machine. The length of this seam should be equal to the depth of the bag. Snip the turnings as in Fig. 131b. Turn the bag right side out as in Fig. 131c and join the two raw edges of the pocket piece. Turn the pocket piece up onto the right side, mark out the position of the pockets and join to the sides of the bag by machining as in Fig. 131d. Cut a piece of cardboard for the base, then cut a piece of woven fabric the size of base plus $\frac{3}{8}''$ on all sides. Place in a running stitch on the outer edge of fabric and place the cardboard onto the material (Fig. 131e). Draw up the gathering thread so that the edges of fabric curve over the edge of cardboard (Fig. 131f). Attach the base to the bag; keeping

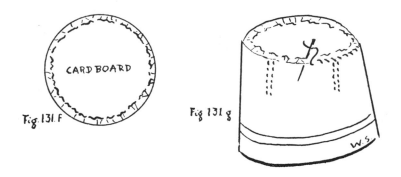

CARDBOARD

Fig. 131. F   Fig 131 g

the bag wrong side out, oversew to the base (Fig. 131g). Make another base as for the previous one, and if short of woven fabric, line with a plain cotton. Turn the bag right side out and place the second base inside it. For this type of bag it will be necessary to stitch a strip of tape $1''$–$1\frac{1}{2}''$ from the top edge of the bag to form a casing as in Fig. 131g. The tape is stitched on the inside of the bag. Make two slots on the right side at the back of the casing, thread through two cords, as this helps for drawing up the bag quickly.

Bags with a base

Plates 1 and 2.   Some bags have a shaped base.   These may be round or oval.   Cut the base piece off the strip of weaving. Join the sides of the bag as in Fig. 131c.   Make the base as for the previous bag and attach to the bag as in Fig. 131f. Make an inner base to hide all raw edges.   Attach the handles to the sides of the bag.   These may be in the form of very thick cord.   Some bags may be lined with plastic or towelling. The seam necessary to join the strip of weaving may be partly hidden by using decorative stitching.   This was done on the beach bag in Plate 1.   This bag has four rows of decorative stitching, which make it difficult to find the seam.

Needle Case

This may be made of woven fabric; cut two pieces of cardboard the size of the needle case.   Cover with the woven fabric and line with felt.   Stitch a strip of flannel inside ready for needles.

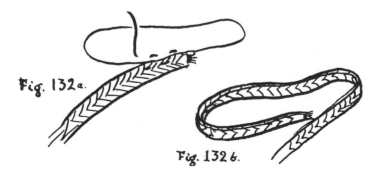

Fig. 132a.

Fig. 132b.

Sandals and Slippers

These may have a lined inner sole.   If so, cut the lining the size of the inner sole plus $\frac{1}{4}''$ all round.   Secure the turnings to the underside of the inner sole by glue or by stitching, using large stitches, drawing the stitches from one side to the other. Stitch the upper to the inner sole, then attach to the sole. The soles may be made of plaited raffia, rope or rubber.

To make plaited raffia soles. Cut out an inner sole of cardboard. Plait lengths of raffia and begin to stitch the narrow edge of the plaited raffia to the cardboard (Fig. 132a). Keep winding the raffia round and round, working from the outside towards the inside of the sole. Make sure that the rows are stitched close together.

PLATE 8

Patterns in left-hand column, reading from top to bottom, are a,
b, c, d and e; in right-hand column, f, g, h, i and j (*see* pages 59, 60).

INDEX

A CATALOGUE OF SELECTED DOVER BOOKS
IN ALL FIELDS OF INTEREST

A CATALOGUE OF SELECTED DOVER BOOKS
IN ALL FIELDS OF INTEREST

LEATHER TOOLING AND CARVING, Chris H. Groneman. One of few books concentrating on tooling and carving, with complete instructions and grid designs for 39 projects ranging from bookmarks to bags. 148 illustrations. 111pp. 7⅞ x 10.
23061-9 Pa. $2.50

THE CODEX NUTTALL, A PICTURE MANUSCRIPT FROM ANCIENT MEXICO, as first edited by Zelia Nuttall. Only inexpensive edition, in full color, of a pre-Columbian Mexican (Mixtec) book. 88 color plates show kings, gods, heroes, temples, sacrifices. New explanatory, historical introduction by Arthur G. Miller. 96pp. 11⅜ x 8½.
23168-2 Pa. $7.50

AMERICAN PRIMITIVE PAINTING, Jean Lipman. Classic collection of an enduring American tradition. 109 plates, 8 in full color—portraits, landscapes, Biblical and historical scenes, etc., showing family groups, farm life, and so on. 80pp. of lucid text. 8⅜ x 11¼.
22815-0 Pa. $4.00

WILL BRADLEY: HIS GRAPHIC ART, edited by Clarence P. Hornung. Striking collection of work by foremost practitioner of Art Nouveau in America: posters, cover designs, sample pages, advertisements, other illustrations. 97 plates, including 8 in full color and 19 in two colors. 97pp. 9⅜ x 12¼.
20701-3 Pa. $4.00
22120-2 Clothbd. $10.00

THE UNDERGROUND SKETCHBOOK OF JAN FAUST, Jan Faust. 101 bitter, horrifying, black-humorous, penetrating sketches on sex, war, greed, various liberations, etc. Sometimes sexual, but not pornographic. Not for prudish. 101pp. 6½ x 9¼.
22740-5 Pa. $1.50

THE GIBSON GIRL AND HER AMERICA, Charles Dana Gibson. 155 finest drawings of effervescent world of 1900-1910: the Gibson Girl and her loves, amusements, adventures, Mr. Pipp, etc. Selected by E. Gillon; introduction by Henry Pitz. 144pp. 8¼ x 11⅜.
21986-0 Pa. $3.50

STAINED GLASS CRAFT, J.A.F. Divine, G. Blachford. One of the very few books that tell the beginner exactly what he needs to know: planning cuts, making shapes, avoiding design weaknesses, fitting glass, etc. 93 illustrations. 115pp.
22812-6 Pa. $1.50

CREATIVE LITHOGRAPHY AND HOW TO DO IT, Grant Arnold. Lithography as art form: working directly on stone, transfer of drawings, lithotint, mezzotint, color printing; also metal plates. Detailed, thorough. 27 illustrations. 214pp.
21208-4 Pa. $3.00

DESIGN MOTIFS OF ANCIENT MEXICO, Jorge Enciso. Vigorous, powerful ceramic stamp impressions — Maya, Aztec, Toltec, Olmec. Serpents, gods, priests, dancers, etc. 153pp. 6⅛ x 9¼.
20084-1 Pa. $2.50

AMERICAN INDIAN DESIGN AND DECORATION, Leroy Appleton. Full text, plus more than 700 precise drawings of Inca, Maya, Aztec, Pueblo, Plains, NW Coast basketry, sculpture, painting, pottery, sand paintings, metal, etc. 4 plates in color. 279pp. 8⅜ x 11¼.
22704-9 Pa. $4.50

CHINESE LATTICE DESIGNS, Daniel S. Dye. Incredibly beautiful geometric designs: circles, voluted, simple dissections, etc. Inexhaustible source of ideas, motifs. 1239 illustrations. 469pp. 6⅛ x 9¼.
23096-1 Pa. $5.00

JAPANESE DESIGN MOTIFS, Matsuya Co. Mon, or heraldic designs. Over 4000 typical, beautiful designs: birds, animals, flowers, swords, fans, geometric; all beautifully stylized. 213pp. 11⅜ x 8¼.
22874-6 Pa. $5.00

PERSPECTIVE, Jan Vredeman de Vries. 73 perspective plates from 1604 edition; buildings, townscapes, stairways, fantastic scenes. Remarkable for beauty, surrealistic atmosphere; real eye-catchers. Introduction by Adolf Placzek. 74pp. 11⅜ x 8¼.
20186-4 Pa. $2.75

EARLY AMERICAN DESIGN MOTIFS. Suzanne E. Chapman. 497 motifs, designs, from painting on wood, ceramics, appliqué, glassware, samplers, metal work, etc. Florals, landscapes, birds and animals, geometrics, letters, etc. Inexhaustible. Enlarged edition. 138pp. 8⅜ x 11¼.
22985-8 Pa. $3.50
23084-8 Clothbd. $7.95

VICTORIAN STENCILS FOR DESIGN AND DECORATION, edited by E.V. Gillon, Jr. 113 wonderful ornate Victorian pieces from German sources; florals, geometrics; borders, corner pieces; bird motifs, etc. 64pp. 9⅜ x 12¼.
21995-X Pa. $2.75

ART NOUVEAU: AN ANTHOLOGY OF DESIGN AND ILLUSTRATION FROM THE STUDIO, edited by E.V. Gillon, Jr. Graphic arts: book jackets, posters, engravings, illustrations, decorations; Crane, Beardsley, Bradley and many others. Inexhaustible. 92pp. 8⅛ x 11.
22388-4 Pa. $2.50

ORIGINAL ART DECO DESIGNS, William Rowe. First-rate, highly imaginative modern Art Deco frames, borders, compositions, alphabets, florals, insectals, Wurlitzer-types, etc. Much finest modern Art Deco. 80 plates, 8 in color. 8⅜ x 11¼.
22567-4 Pa. $3.00

HANDBOOK OF DESIGNS AND DEVICES, Clarence P. Hornung. Over 1800 basic geometric designs based on circle, triangle, square, scroll, cross, etc. Largest such collection in existence. 261pp.
20125-2 Pa. $2.50

150 MASTERPIECES OF DRAWING, edited by Anthony Toney. 150 plates, early 15th century to end of 18th century; Rembrandt, Michelangelo, Dürer, Fragonard, Watteau, Wouwerman, many others. 150pp. 8⅜ x 11¼. 21032-4 Pa. $3.50

THE GOLDEN AGE OF THE POSTER, Hayward and Blanche Cirker. 70 extraordinary posters in full colors, from Maîtres de l'Affiche, Mucha, Lautrec, Bradley, Cheret, Beardsley, many others. 9⅜ x 12¼. 22753-7 Pa. $4.95
21718-3 Clothbd. $7.95

SIMPLICISSIMUS, selection, translations and text by Stanley Appelbaum. 180 satirical drawings, 16 in full color, from the famous German weekly magazine in the years 1896 to 1926. 24 artists included: Grosz, Kley, Pascin, Kubin, Kollwitz, plus Heine, Thöny, Bruno Paul, others. 172pp. 8½ x 12¼. 23098-8 Pa. $5.00
23099-6 Clothbd. $10.00

THE EARLY WORK OF AUBREY BEARDSLEY, Aubrey Beardsley. 157 plates, 2 in color: Manon Lescaut, Madame Bovary, Morte d'Arthur, Salome, other. Introduction by H. Marillier. 175pp. 8½ x 11. 21816-3 Pa. $3.50

THE LATER WORK OF AUBREY BEARDSLEY, Aubrey Beardsley. Exotic masterpieces of full maturity: Venus and Tannhäuser, Lysistrata, Rape of the Lock, Volpone, Savoy material, etc. 174 plates, 2 in color. 176pp. 8½ x 11. 21817-1 Pa. $4.00

DRAWINGS OF WILLIAM BLAKE, William Blake. 92 plates from Book of Job, Divine Comedy, Paradise Lost, visionary heads, mythological figures, Laocoön, etc. Selection, introduction, commentary by Sir Geoffrey Keynes. 178pp. 8½ x 11. 22303-5 Pa. $3.50

LONDON: A PILGRIMAGE, Gustave Doré, Blanchard Jerrold. Squalor, riches, misery, beauty of mid-Victorian metropolis; 55 wonderful plates, 125 other illustrations, full social, cultural text by Jerrold. 191pp. of text. 8⅛ x 11. 22306-X Pa. $5.00

THE COMPLETE WOODCUTS OF ALBRECHT DÜRER, edited by Dr. W. Kurth. 346 in all: Old Testament, St. Jerome, Passion, Life of Virgin, Apocalypse, many others. Introduction by Campbell Dodgson. 285pp. 8½ x 12¼. 21097-9 Pa. $6.00

THE DISASTERS OF WAR, Francisco Goya. 83 etchings record horrors of Napoleonic wars in Spain and war in general. Reprint of 1st edition, plus 3 additional plates. Introduction by Philip Hofer. 97pp. 9⅜ x 8¼. 21872-4 Pa. $3.00

ENGRAVINGS OF HOGARTH, William Hogarth. 101 of Hogarth's greatest works: Rake's Progress, Harlot's Progress, Illustrations for Hudibras, Midnight Modern Conversation, Before and After, Beer Street and Gin Lane, many more. Full commentary. 256pp. 11 x 14. 22479-1 Pa. $7.00
23023-6 Clothbd. $13.50

PRIMITIVE ART, Franz Boas. Great anthropologist on ceramics, textiles, wood, stone, metal, etc.; patterns, technology, symbols, styles. All areas, but fullest on Northwest Coast Indians. 350 illustrations. 378pp. 20025-6 Pa. $3.50

MOTHER GOOSE'S MELODIES. Facsimile of fabulously rare Munroe and Francis "copyright 1833" Boston edition. Familiar and unusual rhymes, wonderful old woodcut illustrations. Edited by E.F. Bleiler. 128pp. 4½ x 6⅜. 22577-1 Pa. $1.00

MOTHER GOOSE IN HIEROGLYPHICS. Favorite nursery rhymes presented in rebus form for children. Fascinating 1849 edition reproduced in toto, with key. Introduction by E.F. Bleiler. About 400 woodcuts. 64pp. 6⅞ x 5¼. 20745-5 Pa. $1.00

PETER PIPER'S PRACTICAL PRINCIPLES OF PLAIN & PERFECT PRONUNCIATION. Alliterative jingles and tongue-twisters. Reproduction in full of 1830 first American edition. 25 spirited woodcuts. 32pp. 4½ x 6⅜. 22560-7 Pa. $1.00

MARMADUKE MULTIPLY'S MERRY METHOD OF MAKING MINOR MATHEMATICIANS. Fellow to Peter Piper, it teaches multiplication table by catchy rhymes and woodcuts. 1841 Munroe & Francis edition. Edited by E.F. Bleiler. 103pp. 4⅝ x 6.
22773-1 Pa. $1.25
20171-6 Clothbd. $3.00

THE NIGHT BEFORE CHRISTMAS, Clement Moore. Full text, and woodcuts from original 1848 book. Also critical, historical material. 19 illustrations. 40pp. 4⅝ x 6. 22797-9 Pa. $1.00

THE KING OF THE GOLDEN RIVER, John Ruskin. Victorian children's classic of three brothers, their attempts to reach the Golden River, what becomes of them. Facsimile of original 1889 edition. 22 illustrations. 56pp. 4⅝ x 6⅜.
20066-3 Pa. $1.25

DREAMS OF THE RAREBIT FIEND, Winsor McCay. Pioneer cartoon strip, unexcelled for beauty, imagination, in 60 full sequences. Incredible technical virtuosity, wonderful visual wit. Historical introduction. 62pp. 8⅜ x 11¼. 21347-1 Pa. $2.50

THE KATZENJAMMER KIDS, Rudolf Dirks. In full color, 14 strips from 1906-7; full of imagination, characteristic humor. Classic of great historical importance. Introduction by August Derleth. 32pp. 9¼ x 12¼. 23005-8 Pa. $2.00

LITTLE ORPHAN ANNIE AND LITTLE ORPHAN ANNIE IN COSMIC CITY, Harold Gray. Two great sequences from the early strips: our curly-haired heroine defends the Warbucks' financial empire and, then, takes on meanie Phineas P. Pinchpenny. Leapin' lizards! 178pp. 6⅛ x 8⅜. 23107-0 Pa. $2.00

WHEN A FELLER NEEDS A FRIEND, Clare Briggs. 122 cartoons by one of the greatest newspaper cartoonists of the early 20th century — about growing up, making a living, family life, daily frustrations and occasional triumphs. 121pp. 8½ x 9½.
23148-8 Pa. $2.50

THE BEST OF GLUYAS WILLIAMS. 100 drawings by one of America's finest cartoonists: The Day a Cake of Ivory Soap Sank at Proctor & Gamble's, At the Life Insurance Agents' Banquet, and many other gems from the 20's and 30's. 118pp. 8⅜ x 11¼. 22737-5 Pa. $2.50

THE BEST DR. THORNDYKE DETECTIVE STORIES, R. Austin Freeman. The Case of Oscar Brodski, The Moabite Cipher, and 5 other favorites featuring the great scientific detective, plus his long-believed-lost first adventure — 31 New Inn — reprinted here for the first time. Edited by E.F. Bleiler. USO 20388-3 Pa. $3.00

BEST "THINKING MACHINE" DETECTIVE STORIES, Jacques Futrelle. The Problem of Cell 13 and 11 other stories about Prof. Augustus S.F.X. Van Dusen, including two "lost" stories. First reprinting of several. Edited by E.F. Bleiler. 241pp.
20537-1 Pa. $3.00

UNCLE SILAS, J. Sheridan LeFanu. Victorian Gothic mystery novel, considered by many best of period, even better than Collins or Dickens. Wonderful psychological terror. Introduction by Frederick Shroyer. 436pp. 21715-9 Pa. $4.00

BEST DR. POGGIOLI DETECTIVE STORIES, T.S. Stribling. 15 best stories from EQMM and The Saint offer new adventures in Mexico, Florida, Tennessee hills as Poggioli unravels mysteries and combats Count Jalacki. 217pp. 23227-1 Pa. $3.00

EIGHT DIME NOVELS, selected with an introduction by E.F. Bleiler. Adventures of Old King Brady, Frank James, Nick Carter, Deadwood Dick, Buffalo Bill, The Steam Man, Frank Merriwell, and Horatio Alger — 1877 to 1905. Important, entertaining popular literature in facsimile reprint, with original covers. 190pp. 9 x 12. 22975-0 Pa. $3.50

ALICE'S ADVENTURES UNDER GROUND, Lewis Carroll. Facsimile of ms. Carroll gave Alice Liddell in 1864. Different in many ways from final Alice. Handlettered, illustrated by Carroll. Introduction by Martin Gardner. 128pp. 21482-6 Pa. $1.50

ALICE IN WONDERLAND COLORING BOOK, Lewis Carroll. Pictures by John Tenniel. Large-size versions of the famous illustrations of Alice, Cheshire Cat, Mad Hatter and all the others, waiting for your crayons. Abridged text. 36 illustrations. 64pp. 8¼ x 11. 22853-3 Pa. $1.50

AVENTURES D'ALICE AU PAYS DES MERVEILLES, Lewis Carroll. Bué's translation of "Alice" into French, supervised by Carroll himself. Novel way to learn language. (No English text.) 42 Tenniel illustrations. 196pp. 22836-3 Pa. $2.50

MYTHS AND FOLK TALES OF IRELAND, Jeremiah Curtin. 11 stories that are Irish versions of European fairy tales and 9 stories from the Fenian cycle — 20 tales of legend and magic that comprise an essential work in the history of folklore. 256pp. 22430-9 Pa. $3.00

EAST O' THE SUN AND WEST O' THE MOON, George W. Dasent. Only full edition of favorite, wonderful Norwegian fairytales — Why the Sea is Salt, Boots and the Troll, etc. — with 77 illustrations by Kittelsen & Werenskiöld. 418pp.
22521-6 Pa. $4.00

PERRAULT'S FAIRY TALES, Charles Perrault and Gustave Doré. Original versions of Cinderella, Sleeping Beauty, Little Red Riding Hood, etc. in best translation, with 34 wonderful illustrations by Gustave Doré. 117pp. 8⅛ x 11. 22311-6 Pa. $2.50

EARLY NEW ENGLAND GRAVESTONE RUBBINGS, Edmund V. Gillon, Jr. 43 photographs, 226 rubbings show heavily symbolic, macabre, sometimes humorous primitive American art. Up to early 19th century. 207pp. 8⅜ x 11¼.
21380-3 Pa. $4.00

L.J.M. DAGUERRE: THE HISTORY OF THE DIORAMA AND THE DAGUERREOTYPE, Helmut and Alison Gernsheim. Definitive account. Early history, life and work of Daguerre; discovery of daguerreotype process; diffusion abroad; other early photography. 124 illustrations. 226pp. 6⅙ x 9¼. 22290-X Pa. $4.00

PHOTOGRAPHY AND THE AMERICAN SCENE, Robert Taft. The basic book on American photography as art, recording form, 1839-1889. Development, influence on society, great photographers, types (portraits, war, frontier, etc.), whatever else needed. Inexhaustible. Illustrated with 322 early photos, daguerreotypes, tintypes, stereo slides, etc. 546pp. 6⅛ x 9¼. 21201-7 Pa. $5.95

PHOTOGRAPHIC SKETCHBOOK OF THE CIVIL WAR, Alexander Gardner. Reproduction of 1866 volume with 100 on-the-field photographs: Manassas, Lincoln on battlefield, slave pens, etc. Introduction by E.F. Bleiler. 224pp. 10¾ x 9.
22731-6 Pa. $5.00

THE MOVIES: A PICTURE QUIZ BOOK, Stanley Appelbaum & Hayward Cirker. Match stars with their movies, name actors and actresses, test your movie skill with 241 stills from 236 great movies, 1902-1959. Indexes of performers and films. 128pp. 8⅜ x 9¼. 20222-4 Pa. $2.50

THE TALKIES, Richard Griffith. Anthology of features, articles from Photoplay, 1928-1940, reproduced complete. Stars, famous movies, technical features, fabulous ads, etc.; Garbo, Chaplin, King Kong, Lubitsch, etc. 4 color plates, scores of illustrations. 327pp. 8⅜ x 11¼. 22762-6 Pa. $6.95

THE MOVIE MUSICAL FROM VITAPHONE TO "42ND STREET," edited by Miles Kreuger. Relive the rise of the movie musical as reported in the pages of Photoplay magazine (1926-1933): every movie review, cast list, ad, and record review; every significant feature article, production still, biography, forecast, and gossip story. Profusely illustrated. 367pp. 8⅜ x 11¼. 23154-2 Pa. $6.95

JOHANN SEBASTIAN BACH, Philipp Spitta. Great classic of biography, musical commentary, with hundreds of pieces analyzed. Also good for Bach's contemporaries. 450 musical examples. Total of 1799pp.
EUK 22278-0, 22279-9 Clothbd., Two vol. set $25.00

BEETHOVEN AND HIS NINE SYMPHONIES, Sir George Grove. Thorough history, analysis, commentary on symphonies and some related pieces. For either beginner or advanced student. 436 musical passages. 407pp. 20334-4 Pa. $4.00

MOZART AND HIS PIANO CONCERTOS, Cuthbert Girdlestone. The only full-length study. Detailed analyses of all 21 concertos, sources; 417 musical examples. 509pp. 21271-8 Pa. $4.50

THE FITZWILLIAM VIRGINAL BOOK, edited by J. Fuller Maitland, W.B. Squire. Famous early 17th century collection of keyboard music, 300 works by Morley, Byrd, Bull, Gibbons, etc. Modern notation. Total of 938pp. 8⅜ x 11.
ECE 21068-5, 21069-3 Pa., Two vol. set $14.00

COMPLETE STRING QUARTETS, Wolfgang A. Mozart. Breitkopf and Härtel edition. All 23 string quartets plus alternate slow movement to K156. Study score. 277pp. 9⅜ x 12¼. 22372-8 Pa. $6.00

COMPLETE SONG CYCLES, Franz Schubert. Complete piano, vocal music of Die Schöne Müllerin, Die Winterreise, Schwanengesang. Also Drinker English singing translations. Breitkopf and Härtel edition. 217pp. 9⅜ x 12¼.
22649-2 Pa. $4.50

THE COMPLETE PRELUDES AND ETUDES FOR PIANOFORTE SOLO, Alexander Scriabin. All the preludes and etudes including many perfectly spun miniatures. Edited by K.N. Igumnov and Y.I. Mil'shteyn. 250pp. 9 x 12. 22919-X Pa. $5.00

TRISTAN UND ISOLDE, Richard Wagner. Full orchestral score with complete instrumentation. Do not confuse with piano reduction. Commentary by Felix Mottl, great Wagnerian conductor and scholar. Study score. 655pp. 8⅛ x 11.
22915-7 Pa. $10.00

FAVORITE SONGS OF THE NINETIES, ed. Robert Fremont. Full reproduction, including covers, of 88 favorites: Ta-Ra-Ra-Boom-De-Aye, The Band Played On, Bird in a Gilded Cage, Under the Bamboo Tree, After the Ball, etc. 401pp. 9 x 12.
EBE 21536-9 Pa. $6.95

SOUSA'S GREAT MARCHES IN PIANO TRANSCRIPTION: ORIGINAL SHEET MUSIC OF 23 WORKS, John Philip Sousa. Selected by Lester S. Levy. Playing edition includes: The Stars and Stripes Forever, The Thunderer, The Gladiator, King Cotton, Washington Post, much more. 24 illustrations. 111pp. 9 x 12.
USO 23132-1 Pa. $3.50

CLASSIC PIANO RAGS, selected with an introduction by Rudi Blesh. Best ragtime music (1897-1922) by Scott Joplin, James Scott, Joseph F. Lamb, Tom Turpin, 9 others. Printed from best original sheet music, plus covers. 364pp. 9 x 12.
EBE 20469-3 Pa. $6.95

ANALYSIS OF CHINESE CHARACTERS, C.D. Wilder, J.H. Ingram. 1000 most important characters analyzed according to primitives, phonetics, historical development. Traditional method offers mnemonic aid to beginner, intermediate student of Chinese, Japanese. 365pp. 23045-7 Pa. $4.00

MODERN CHINESE: A BASIC COURSE, Faculty of Peking University. Self study, classroom course in modern Mandarin. Records contain phonetics, vocabulary, sentences, lessons. 249 page book contains all recorded text, translations, grammar, vocabulary, exercises. Best course on market. 3 12" 33⅓ monaural records, book, album. 98832-5 Set $12.50

MANUAL OF THE TREES OF NORTH AMERICA, Charles S. Sargent. The basic survey of every native tree and tree-like shrub, 717 species in all. Extremely full descriptions, information on habitat, growth, locales, economics, etc. Necessary to every serious tree lover. Over 100 finding keys. 783 illustrations. Total of 986pp.
20277-1, 20278-X Pa., Two vol. set $8.00

BIRDS OF THE NEW YORK AREA, John Bull. Indispensable guide to more than 400 species within a hundred-mile radius of Manhattan. Information on range, status, breeding, migration, distribution trends, etc. Foreword by Roger Tory Peterson. 17 drawings; maps. 540pp.
23222-0 Pa. $6.00

THE SEA-BEACH AT EBB-TIDE, Augusta Foote Arnold. Identify hundreds of marine plants and animals: algae, seaweeds, squids, crabs, corals, etc. Descriptions cover food, life cycle, size, shape, habitat. Over 600 drawings. 490pp.
21949-6 Pa. $5.00

THE MOTH BOOK, William J. Holland. Identify more than 2,000 moths of North America. General information, precise species descriptions. 623 illustrations plus 48 color plates show almost all species, full size. 1968 edition. Still the basic book. Total of 551pp. 6½ x 9¼.
21948-8 Pa. $6.00

AN INTRODUCTION TO THE REPTILES AND AMPHIBIANS OF THE UNITED STATES, Percy A. Morris. All lizards, crocodiles, turtles, snakes, toads, frogs; life history, identification, habits, suitability as pets, etc. Non-technical, but sound and broad. 130 photos. 253pp.
22982-3 Pa. $3.00

OLD NEW YORK IN EARLY PHOTOGRAPHS, edited by Mary Black. Your only chance to see New York City as it was 1853-1906, through 196 wonderful photographs from N.Y. Historical Society. Great Blizzard, Lincoln's funeral procession, great buildings. 228pp. 9 x 12.
22907-6 Pa. $6.00

THE AMERICAN REVOLUTION, A PICTURE SOURCEBOOK, John Grafton. Wonderful Bicentennial picture source, with 411 illustrations (contemporary and 19th century) showing battles, personalities, maps, events, flags, posters, soldier's life, ships, etc. all captioned and explained. A wonderful browsing book, supplement to other historical reading. 160pp. 9 x 12.
23226-3 Pa. $4.00

PERSONAL NARRATIVE OF A PILGRIMAGE TO AL-MADINAH AND MECCAH, Richard Burton. Great travel classic by remarkably colorful personality. Burton, disguised as a Moroccan, visited sacred shrines of Islam, narrowly escaping death. Wonderful observations of Islamic life, customs, personalities. 47 illustrations. Total of 959pp.
21217-3, 21218-1 Pa., Two vol. set $10.00

INCIDENTS OF TRAVEL IN CENTRAL AMERICA, CHIAPAS, AND YUCATAN, John L. Stephens. Almost single-handed discovery of Maya culture; exploration of ruined cities, monuments, temples; customs of Indians. 115 drawings. 892pp.
22404-X, 22405-8 Pa., Two vol. set $8.00

CONSTRUCTION OF AMERICAN FURNITURE TREASURES, Lester Margon. 344 detail drawings, complete text on constructing exact reproductions of 38 early American masterpieces: Hepplewhite sideboard, Duncan Phyfe drop-leaf table, mantel clock, gate-leg dining table, Pa. German cupboard, more. 38 plates. 54 photographs. 168pp. 8⅜ x 11¼. 23056-2 Pa. $4.00

JEWELRY MAKING AND DESIGN, Augustus F. Rose, Antonio Cirino. Professional secrets revealed in thorough, practical guide: tools, materials, processes; rings, brooches, chains, cast pieces, enamelling, setting stones, etc. Do not confuse with skimpy introductions: beginner can use, professional can learn from it. Over 200 illustrations. 306pp. 21750-7 Pa. $3.00

METALWORK AND ENAMELLING, Herbert Maryon. Generally coneeded best all-around book. Countless trade secrets: materials, tools, soldering, filigree, setting, inlay, niello, repoussé, casting, polishing, etc. For beginner or expert. Author was foremost British expert. 330 illustrations. 335pp. 22702-2 Pa. $3.50

WEAVING WITH FOOT-POWER LOOMS, Edward F. Worst. Setting up a loom, beginning to weave, constructing equipment, using dyes, more, plus over 285 drafts of traditional patterns including Colonial and Swedish weaves. More than 200 other figures. For beginning and advanced. 275pp. 8¾ x 6⅜. 23064-3 Pa. $4.00

WEAVING A NAVAJO BLANKET, Gladys A. Reichard. Foremost anthropologist studied under Navajo women, reveals every step in process from wool, dyeing, spinning, setting up loom, designing, weaving. Much history, symbolism. With this book you could make one yourself. 97 illustrations. 222pp. 22992-0 Pa. $3.00

NATURAL DYES AND HOME DYEING, Rita J. Adrosko. Use natural ingredients: bark, flowers, leaves, lichens, insects etc. Over 135 specific recipes from historical sources for cotton, wool, other fabrics. Genuine premodern handicrafts. 12 illustrations. 160pp. 22688-3 Pa. $2.00

THE HAND DECORATION OF FABRICS, Francis J. Kafka. Outstanding, profusely illustrated guide to stenciling, batik, block printing, tie dyeing, freehand painting, silk screen printing, and novelty decoration. 356 illustrations. 198pp. 6 x 9. 21401-X Pa. $3.00

THOMAS NAST: CARTOONS AND ILLUSTRATIONS, with text by Thomas Nast St. Hill. Father of American political cartooning. Cartoons that destroyed Tweed Ring; inflation, free love, church and state; original Republican elephant and Democratic donkey; Santa Claus; more. 117 illustrations. 146pp. 9 x 12.
22983-1 Pa. $4.00
23067-8 Clothbd. $8.50

FREDERIC REMINGTON: 173 DRAWINGS AND ILLUSTRATIONS. Most famous of the Western artists, most responsible for our myths about the American West in its untamed days. Complete reprinting of Drawings of Frederic Remington (1897), plus other selections. 4 additional drawings in color on covers. 140pp. 9 x 12.
20714-5 Pa. $3.95

How to Solve Chess Problems, Kenneth S. Howard. Practical suggestions on problem solving for very beginners. 58 two-move problems, 46 3-movers, 8 4-movers for practice, plus hints. 171pp. 20748-X Pa. $2.00

A Guide to Fairy Chess, Anthony Dickins. 3-D chess, 4-D chess, chess on a cylindrical board, reflecting pieces that bounce off edges, cooperative chess, retrograde chess, maximummers, much more. Most based on work of great Dawson. Full handbook, 100 problems. 66pp. 7⅞ x 10¾. 22687-5 Pa. $2.00

Win at Backgammon, Millard Hopper. Best opening moves, running game, blocking game, back game, tables of odds, etc. Hopper makes the game clear enough for anyone to play, and win. 43 diagrams. 111pp. 22894-0 Pa. $1.50

Bidding a Bridge Hand, Terence Reese. Master player "thinks out loud" the binding of 75 hands that defy point count systems. Organized by bidding problem—no-fit situations, overbidding, underbidding, cueing your defense, etc. 254pp. EBE 22830-4 Pa. $2.50

The Precision Bidding System in Bridge, C.C. Wei, edited by Alan Truscott. Inventor of precision bidding presents average hands and hands from actual play, including games from 1969 Bermuda Bowl where system emerged. 114 exercises. 116pp. 21171-1 Pa. $1.75

Learn Magic, Henry Hay. 20 simple, easy-to-follow lessons on magic for the new magician: illusions, card tricks, silks, sleights of hand, coin manipulations, escapes, and more —all with a minimum amount of equipment. Final chapter explains the great stage illusions. 92 illustrations. 285pp. 21238-6 Pa. $2.95

The New Magician's Manual, Walter B. Gibson. Step-by-step instructions and clear illustrations guide the novice in mastering 36 tricks; much equipment supplied on 16 pages of cut-out materials. 36 additional tricks. 64 illustrations. 159pp. 6⅝ x 10. 23113-5 Pa. $3.00

Professional Magic for Amateurs, Walter B. Gibson. 50 easy, effective tricks used by professionals —cards, string, tumblers, handkerchiefs, mental magic, etc. 63 illustrations. 223pp. 23012-0 Pa. $2.50

Card Manipulations, Jean Hugard. Very rich collection of manipulations; has taught thousands of fine magicians tricks that are really workable, eye-catching. Easily followed, serious work. Over 200 illustrations. 163pp. 20539-8 Pa. $2.00

Abbott's Encyclopedia of Rope Tricks for Magicians, Stewart James. Complete reference book for amateur and professional magicians containing more than 150 tricks involving knots, penetrations, cut and restored rope, etc. 510 illustrations. Reprint of 3rd edition. 400pp. 23206-9 Pa. $3.50

The Secrets of Houdini, J.C. Cannell. Classic study of Houdini's incredible magic, exposing closely-kept professional secrets and revealing, in general terms, the whole art of stage magic. 67 illustrations. 279pp. 22913-0 Pa. $2.50

THE MAGIC MOVING PICTURE BOOK, Bliss, Sands & Co. The pictures in this book move! Volcanoes erupt, a house burns, a serpentine dancer wiggles her way through a number. By using a specially ruled acetate screen provided, you can obtain these and 15 other startling effects. Originally "The Motograph Moving Picture Book." 32pp. 8¼ x 11.   23224-7 Pa. $1.75

STRING FIGURES AND HOW TO MAKE THEM, Caroline F. Jayne. Fullest, clearest instructions on string figures from around world: Eskimo, Navajo, Lapp, Europe, more. Cats cradle, moving spear, lightning, stars. Introduction by A.C. Haddon. 950 illustrations. 407pp.   20152-X Pa. $3.00

PAPER FOLDING FOR BEGINNERS, William D. Murray and Francis J. Rigney. Clearest book on market for making origami sail boats, roosters, frogs that move legs, cups, bonbon boxes. 40 projects. More than 275 illustrations. Photographs. 94pp.
                                     20713-7 Pa. $1.25

INDIAN SIGN LANGUAGE, William Tomkins. Over 525 signs developed by Sioux, Blackfoot, Cheyenne, Arapahoe and other tribes. Written instructions and diagrams: how to make words, construct sentences. Also 290 pictographs of Sioux and Ojibway tribes. 111pp. 6⅛ x 9¼.   22029-X Pa. $1.50

BOOMERANGS: HOW TO MAKE AND THROW THEM, Bernard S. Mason. Easy to make and throw, dozens of designs: cross-stick, pinwheel, boomabird, tumblestick, Australian curved stick boomerang. Complete throwing instructions. All safe. 99pp.   23028-7 Pa. $1.50

25 KITES THAT FLY, Leslie Hunt. Full, easy to follow instructions for kites made from inexpensive materials. Many novelties. Reeling, raising, designing your own. 70 illustrations. 110pp.   22550-X Pa. $1.25

TRICKS AND GAMES ON THE POOL TABLE, Fred Herrmann. 79 tricks and games, some solitaires, some for 2 or more players, some competitive; mystifying shots and throws, unusual carom, tricks involving cork, coins, a hat, more. 77 figures. 95pp.   21814-7 Pa. $1.25

WOODCRAFT AND CAMPING, Bernard S. Mason. How to make a quick emergency shelter, select woods that will burn immediately, make do with limited supplies, etc. Also making many things out of wood, rawhide, bark, at camp. Formerly titled Woodcraft. 295 illustrations. 580pp.   21951-8 Pa. $4.00

AN INTRODUCTION TO CHESS MOVES AND TACTICS SIMPLY EXPLAINED, Leonard Barden. Informal intermediate introduction: reasons for moves, tactics, openings, traps, positional play, endgame. Isolates patterns. 102pp. USO 21210-6 Pa. $1.35

LASKER'S MANUAL OF CHESS, Dr. Emanuel Lasker. Great world champion offers very thorough coverage of all aspects of chess. Combinations, position play, openings, endgame, aesthetics of chess, philosophy of struggle, much more. Filled with analyzed games. 390pp.   20640-8 Pa. $3.50

CATALOGUE OF DOVER BOOKS

SLEEPING BEAUTY, illustrated by Arthur Rackham. Perhaps the fullest, most delightful version ever, told by C.S. Evans. Rackham's best work. 49 illustrations. 110pp. 7⅞ x 10¾. 22756-1 Pa. $2.00

THE WONDERFUL WIZARD OF OZ, L. Frank Baum. Facsimile in full color of America's finest children's classic. Introduction by Martin Gardner. 143 illustrations by W.W. Denslow. 267pp. 20691-2 Pa. $2.50

GOOPS AND HOW TO BE THEM, Gelett Burgess. Classic tongue-in-cheek masquerading as etiquette book. 87 verses, 170 cartoons as Goops demonstrate virtues of table manners, neatness, courtesy, more. 88pp. 6½ x 9¼. 22233-0 Pa. $1.50

THE BROWNIES, THEIR BOOK, Palmer Cox. Small as mice, cunning as foxes, exuberant, mischievous, Brownies go to zoo, toy shop, seashore, circus, more. 24 verse adventures. 266 illustrations. 144pp. 6⅝ x 9¼. 21265-3 Pa. $1.75

BILLY WHISKERS: THE AUTOBIOGRAPHY OF A GOAT, Frances Trego Montgomery. Escapades of that rambunctious goat. Favorite from turn of the century America. 24 illustrations. 259pp. 22345-0 Pa. $2.75

THE ROCKET BOOK, Peter Newell. Fritz, janitor's kid, sets off rocket in basement of apartment house; an ingenious hole punched through every page traces course of rocket. 22 duotone drawings, verses. 48pp. 6⅞ x 8⅜. 22044-3 Pa. $1.50

PECK'S BAD BOY AND HIS PA, George W. Peck. Complete double-volume of great American childhood classic. Hennery's ingenious pranks against outraged pomposity of pa and the grocery man. 97 illustrations. Introduction by E.F. Bleiler. 347pp. 20497-9 Pa. $2.50

THE TALE OF PETER RABBIT, Beatrix Potter. The inimitable Peter's terrifying adventure in Mr. McGregor's garden, with all 27 wonderful, full-color Potter illustrations. 55pp. 4¼ x 5½. USO 22827-4 Pa. $1.00

THE TALE OF MRS. TIGGY-WINKLE, Beatrix Potter. Your child will love this story about a very special hedgehog and all 27 wonderful, full-color Potter illustrations. 57pp. 4¼ x 5½. USO 20546-0 Pa. $1.00

THE TALE OF BENJAMIN BUNNY, Beatrix Potter. Peter Rabbit's cousin coaxes him back into Mr. McGregor's garden for a whole new set of ̄dventures. A favorite with children. All 27 full-color illustrations. 59pp. 4¼ x 5½. USO 21102-9 Pa. $1.00

THE MERRY ADVENTURES OF ROBIN HOOD, Howard Pyle. Facsimile of original (1883) edition, finest modern version of English outlaw's adventures. 23 illustrations by Pyle. 296pp. 6½ x 9¼. 22043-5 Pa. $2.75

TWO LITTLE SAVAGES, Ernest Thompson Seton. Adventures of two boys who lived as Indians; explaining Indian ways, woodlore, pioneer methods. 293 illustrations. 286pp. 20985-7 Pa. $3.00

CATALOGUE OF DOVER BOOKS

HOUDINI ON MAGIC, Harold Houdini. Edited by Walter Gibson, Morris N. Young. How he escaped; exposés of fake spiritualists; instructions for eye-catching tricks; other fascinating material by and about greatest magician. 155 illustrations. 280pp.   20384-0 Pa. $2.50

HANDBOOK OF THE NUTRITIONAL CONTENTS OF FOOD, U.S. Dept. of Agriculture. Largest, most detailed source of food nutrition information ever prepared. Two mammoth tables: one measuring nutrients in 100 grams of edible portion; the other, in edible portion of 1 pound as purchased. Originally titled Composition of Foods. 190pp. 9 x 12.   21342-0 Pa. $4.00

COMPLETE GUIDE TO HOME CANNING, PRESERVING AND FREEZING, U.S. Dept. of Agriculture. Seven basic manuals with full instructions for jams and jellies; pickles and relishes; canning fruits, vegetables, meat; freezing anything. Really good recipes, exact instructions for optimal results. Save a fortune in food. 156 illustrations. 214pp. 6⅛ x 9¼.   22911-4 Pa. $2.50

THE BREAD TRAY, Louis P. De Gouy. Nearly every bread the cook could buy or make: bread sticks of Italy, fruit breads of Greece, glazed rolls of Vienna, everything from corn pone to croissants. Over 500 recipes altogether. including buns, rolls, muffins, scones, and more. 463pp.   23000-7 Pa. $3.50

CREATIVE HAMBURGER COOKERY, Louis P. De Gouy. 182 unusual recipes for casseroles, meat loaves and hamburgers that turn inexpensive ground meat into memorable main dishes: Arizona chili burgers, burger tamale pie, burger stew, burger corn loaf, burger wine loaf, and more. 120pp.   23001-5 Pa. $1.75

LONG ISLAND SEAFOOD COOKBOOK, J. George Frederick and Jean Joyce. Probably the best American seafood cookbook. Hundreds of recipes. 40 gourmet sauces, 123 recipes using oysters alone! All varieties of fish and seafood amply represented. 324pp.   22677-8 Pa. $3.00

THE EPICUREAN: A COMPLETE TREATISE OF ANALYTICAL AND PRACTICAL STUDIES IN THE CULINARY ART, Charles Ranhofer. Great modern classic. 3,500 recipes from master chef of Delmonico's, turn-of-the-century America's best restaurant. Also explained, many techniques known only to professional chefs. 775 illustrations. 1183pp. 6⅝ x 10.   22680-8 Clothbd. $17.50

THE AMERICAN WINE COOK BOOK, Ted Hatch. Over 700 recipes: old favorites livened up with wine plus many more: Czech fish soup, quince soup, sauce Perigueux, shrimp shortcake, filets Stroganoff, cordon bleu goulash, jambonneau, wine fruit cake, more. 314pp.   22796-0 Pa. $2.50

DELICIOUS VEGETARIAN COOKING, Ivan Baker. Close to 500 delicious and varied recipes: soups, main course dishes (pea, bean, lentil, cheese, vegetable, pasta, and egg dishes), savories, stews, whole-wheat breads and cakes, more. 168pp.
                                                                       USO 22834-7 Pa. $1.75

COOKIES FROM MANY LANDS, Josephine Perry. Crullers, oatmeal cookies, chaux au chocolate, English tea cakes, mandel kuchen, Sacher torte, Danish puff pastry, Swedish cookies — a mouth-watering collection of 223 recipes. 157pp.

22832-0 Pa. $2.00

ROSE RECIPES, Eleanour S. Rohde. How to make sauces, jellies, tarts, salads, pot-pourris, sweet bags, pomanders, perfumes from garden roses; all exact recipes. Century old favorites. 95pp.

22957-2 Pa. $1.25

"OSCAR" OF THE WALDORF'S COOKBOOK, Oscar Tschirky. Famous American chef reveals 3455 recipes that made Waldorf great; cream of French, German, American cooking, in all categories. Full instructions, easy home use. 1896 edition. 907pp. 6⅝ x 9⅜.

20790-0 Clothbd. $15.00

JAMS AND JELLIES, May Byron. Over 500 old-time recipes for delicious jams, jellies, marmalades, preserves, and many other items. Probably the largest jam and jelly book in print. Originally titled May Byron's Jam Book. 276pp.

USO 23130-5 Pa. $3.00

MUSHROOM RECIPES, André L. Simon. 110 recipes for everyday and special cooking. Champignons à la grecque, sole bonne femme, chicken liver croustades, more; 9 basic sauces, 13 ways of cooking mushrooms. 54pp.

USO 20913-X Pa. $1.25

FAVORITE SWEDISH RECIPES, edited by Sam Widenfelt. Prepared in Sweden, offers wonderful, clearly explained Swedish dishes: appetizers, meats, pastry and cookies, other categories. Suitable for American kitchen. 90 photos. 157pp.

23156-9 Pa. $2.00

THE BUCKEYE COOKBOOK, Buckeye Publishing Company. Over 1,000 easy-to-follow, traditional recipes from the American Midwest: bread (100 recipes alone), meat, game, jam, candy, cake, ice cream, and many other categories of cooking. 64 illustrations. From 1883 enlarged edition. 416pp.

23218-2 Pa. $4.00

TWENTY-TWO AUTHENTIC BANQUETS FROM INDIA, Robert H. Christie. Complete, easy-to-do recipes for almost 200 authentic Indian dishes assembled in 22 banquets. Arranged by region. Selected from Banquets of the Nations. 192pp.

23200-X Pa. $2.50

Prices subject to change without notice.
Available at your book dealer or write for free catalogue to Dept. GI, Dover Publications, Inc., 180 Varick St., N.Y., N.Y. 10014. Dover publishes more than 150 books each year on science, elementary and advanced mathematics, biology, music, art, literary history, social sciences and other areas.